CIVIL
AIRLINER
RECOGNITION

6th Edition

Peter R. March

Ian Allan PUBLISHING

CONTENTS

Front cover: The first Boeing 747-400 Freighter for British Airways. *Photography © John M. Dibbs*

Back cover: A 70-seat Avro RJ70 regional jet. *Avro*

Title page: Boeing 777. *PRM*

First published 1987
Second edition 1989
Third edition 1991
Fourth edition 1995
Fifth edition 1997
Sixth edition 1999

ISBN 0 7110 2659 9

© Ian Allan Publishing Ltd 1999

Published by Ian Allan Publishing

an imprint of Ian Allan Publishing Ltd, Terminal House, Shepperton, Surrey TW17 8AS.
Printed by Ian Allan Printing Ltd, Riverdene Business Park, Hersham, Surrey KT12 4RG.
Code: 9907/E

Left:
A long-range DC-10-30 in service
with VARIG of Brazil. *DJM*

This revised sixth edition of *abc Civil Airliner Recognition* has been produced in series with *abc Biz Jets: Business and Corporate Aircraft*, *abc Light Aircraft Recognition* and *abc Classic & Warbird Recognition* and is a companion to *abc Civil Aircraft Markings*. It provides the airport visitor, the airline passenger and the interested spectator with a guide to the fascinating variety of airliners likely to be seen at national and regional airports and flying through our skies.

All of the major types are presented in the established *abc* 'Recognition Series' format according to the number and type of engines, as this is the first and foremost recognition feature. This is followed by basic technical information on one of the variants, the date that the first aircraft (usually the prototype) was flown, production details and an indication of how many of the aircraft are in service and with which airline either currently or in recent years.

The main recognition features are listed and where there are several variants these are also noted. Photographs are used to aid recognition, and distinctive variants are also illustrated where possible.

Where the number of passengers is quoted 'plus crew', this figure relates to 'flight deck crew' only and does not take into account the number of cabin crew normally carried on board the aircraft.

Some older types of aircraft such as the Belfast, Gulfstream I and Yak-40 remain in service in very small numbers. These old airliners have been covered briefly in the final section. To assist in locating specific aircraft by name and/or manufacturer an index and cross-reference has also been provided.

Author

Peter R. March is also author of the following publications:

abc Combat Aircraft Recognition
    (Ian Allan Publishing 1998)
abc Classic & Warbird Recognition
    (Ian Allan Publishing 1996)
abc Biz Jets (Ian Allan Publishing 1996)
abc Military Aircraft Markings
    (Ian Allan Publishing 1999)
abc Light Aircraft Recognition
    (Ian Allan Publishing 1997)
Royal Air Force Almanac (RAFBFE 1994)
Brace by Wire to Fly by Wire (RAFBFE 1998)
Sabre to Stealth (RAFBFE 1997)
Hawk Comes of Age (RAFBFE 1995)
The Real Aviation Enthusiast II (RAFBFE 1995)
Eagles (Weidenfeld & Nicolson 1998)
Freedom of the Skies (Cassell 1999)
    and is Managing Editor of the *Royal Air Force Yearbook* and *USAF Yearbook* series
    (RAF Benevolent Fund Enterprises).

Performance Abbreviations

ehp	equivalent horsepower
eshp	equivalent shaft horsepower
hp	horsepower
km/h	kilometres per hour
kN	kilonewton
kW	kilowatt
mph	miles per hour
shp	shaft horsepower
st	static thrust

Acknowledgements

The author would like to thank Brian Strickland for the detailed research and preparation of the material and Ben Dunnell for inputting the new text and checking the copy.

Photographs

Most of the illustrations in *abc Civil Airliner Recognition* are from the PRM Aviation Photo Library, and credited as follows: Andrew March (APM), Daniel March (DJM), Peter R. March (PRM) and Brian Strickland (BSS). Additional photographs are as credited.

ENGINES

Piston engines

The older piston-engined airliners, such as the 55-year-old Douglas DC-4, have radial engines. More modern aircraft are fitted with in-line piston engines such as the Avco Lycoming or Continental flat-six

Top:
The Douglas DC-4 is powered by two Pratt & Whitney R-2000-25D radial engines. *DJM*

Above:
A modern in-line piston – the Textron Lycoming 0-540-E4C5 here fitted to a Pilatus Britten-Norman BN-2A Islander. *APM*

In the 1960s and 1970s the Rolls-Royce Dart turboprop was widely used for medium and short-range airliners such as the Herald, Fokker F27 and Gulfstream I. The early turboprops like the Dart and the Turbomeca Bastan have been replaced by a new generation of shorter, broader and much more powerful turboprops like the Pratt & Whitney Canada PW120-127 series, Garrett TPE 331 and General Electric CT7 from the USA.

Top:
The Fokker F27 was powered by the Rolls-Royce Dart 532-7 turbo-props. *PRM*

Above centre:
The early HP137 Jetstream 200 was fitted with Turboméca Astazou turbo-props. *PRM*

Below centre:
The BAe Jetstream 31 has the much smaller but more powerful Garrett TPE 331-10. *PRM*

Left:
Current turboprops, driving five or six-blade propellers, include the Pratt & Whitney Canada PW125B used by the Fokker 50. *PRM*

ENGINES
Turbofans

Left:
The early, small diameter Pratt & Whitney JT8D-15A turbofans, as fitted to this Boeing 737-200 series, were noisy and often dirty. *PRM*

Below:
The new-generation turbofans, like these CFM56-3C-1 turbofans on a Boeing 737-300 series, are more powerful, have a larger diameter intake, shorter length and small diameter jet pipe. *PRM*

If nothing more than to meet environmental and noise abatement requirements, turbofans have replaced the old noisy, thirsty (and often dirty) turbojets in most airliners – they are much quieter, more powerful and generally have a larger diameter intake, shorter length and a small diameter jet pipe.

Left:
The new and older generation turbofans. In the foreground a Continental Boeing 737-300 series with CFM56s and in the rear a US Air Boeing 737-200 series with the Pratt & Whitney JT8D-15As. *PRM*

Four-turbojet supersonic airliner

Basic data for Concorde 102

Powerplant: Four Rolls-Royce/SNECMA Olympus 593 Mk 602 (reheat) turbojets of 38,050lb st (169.3kN)
Span: 83ft 10in (25.56m)
Length: 203ft 9in (62.10m)
Max Cruise: 1,336mph (2,179km/h)
Passengers: 100 plus three crew
First aircraft flown: 2 March 1969 (French 001); 9 April 1969 (British 102). Entered service with Air France and British Airways 21 January 1976.
Production: Two prototypes, two pre-production and 14 production aircraft.
Recent/current service: With Air France (five) and British Airways (seven).
Recognition: Underwing-mounted engines in two double nacelles. Slender, low-set delta wing. Narrow fuselage with pointed nose that droops for landing. No tailplane, angular fin and rudder. Very tall stalky undercarriage.
Variants: None

Above:
A British Airways Concorde climbing out after take-off. *PRM*

Left:
Concorde's distinctive delta wing makes it easily recognisable. *PRM*

FOUR-ENGINED JET AIRLINERS

Airbus A340

Four-turbofan very long-range airliner

Basic data for Airbus A340-300

Powerplant: Four CFMI CFM56-5C2 turbofans of 31,200lb st (138.8kN), or CFM56-5C3s of 32,500lb st (145kN)
Span: 197ft 10in (60.30m)
Length: 208ft 11in (63.6m)
Max Cruise: 568mph (914km/h)
Passengers: Up to 440 plus two crew
First aircraft flown: 1 April 1992 (A340-200); 25 October 1991 (A340-300).
Production: First airline delivery in January 1993 (A340-200) and February 1993 (A340-300). 151 delivered with over 115 still on order at end of 1998.
Recent/current service: Entered service in 1993 with Air France. Subsequent service with Air China, Air Lanka, Air Mauritius, Air Portugal, Air Tahiti NUI, Austrian AL, Brunei, Cathay Pacific, China Eastern, China Southwest, Egyptair, Gulf Air, Iberia, Kuwait AW, Lufthansa, Olympic, Sabena, Singapore AL, TAP Air Portugal, THY and Virgin Atlantic.

Recognition: Four underwing podded engines in nacelles protruding forward of the leading edge. Long circular narrow-body fuselage tapering towards the tail. Low-set swept (30°) wings of narrow chord with winglets at the tips and five trailing edge fairings. Tall, swept fin and rudder set forward of tail cone. Swept tailplane with dihedral. Similar to A330 but with four engines.

Variants: A340-200 seating 250-300 passengers, has the longest range of any commercial airliner in service. A340-300 is 14ft (4.3m) longer, seating 300-350 passengers and carrying up to 15.5 tonnes of cargo over 7,000 nautical miles. The A340-500 is the ultra-long-haul version with the R-R Trent 500 engines. A340 Combi is available with a maximum payload of 66 tonnes. Optional engines CFM56-5C3 or -5C4 turbofans. Future plans include a 380-seat A340-600 with a new wing and engines, with a stretched A300 airframe, which is due to fly in January 2001.

FOUR-ENGINED JET AIRLINERS

Antonov An-124 Ruslan

Four-turbofan long-range heavy cargo transport

Basic data for Antonov An-124-100 Ruslan

Powerplant: Four Ivchenko Progress D-18T turbofans of 51,590lb st (229kN)
Span: 240ft 5¾ in (73.30m)
Length: 226ft 8½in (69.10m)
Max Cruise: 537mph (865km/h)
First aircraft flown: 26 December 1982.
Production: Production by late 1998 totalled 50.
Recent/current service with: Aeroflot, Air Foyle, HeavyLift Airlines, Polet, Russian Int'l AL, Titan Cargo, Trans-Charter Airlines, Volga-DNEPR and Moscow AW.
Recognition: The world's largest production aircraft. The configuration is similar to the Lockheed C-5 Galaxy; ie high, swept

Above:
Antonov An-124-100 Ruslan in the colours of Moscow Airways. *PRM*

Below:
HeavyLift An-124 about to land, showing its many-wheel bogie undercarriage. *APM*

wing with four large underslung podded engines. Swept fin and rudder. Low-mounted tailplane. Upward hinged nose loading door, with a rear fuselage ramp/door for simultaneous front and rear loading and unloading. Twenty-four wheels on main undercarriage.
Variants: A re-engined 'westernised' version may be launched with GE CF6-80C2 or Rolls-Royce RB211-524HT turbofans. A new cockpit with modern avionics would allow for a four-man flightdeck crew, instead of the usual six.

FOUR-ENGINED JET AIRLINERS

Avro International Aerospace
RJ70/85/100/115 Avroliner

Avro RJ100 operated by the Swiss airline Crossair. *PRM*

Lufthansa City Line operates the shorter RJ85 version of the Avroliner. *PRM*

Four-turbofan short/medium-range airliner

Basic data for Avro RJ85

Powerplant: Four AlliedSignal LF507-1F turbofans of 7,000lb st (31.14kN)
Span: 86ft 5in (26.34m)
Length: 93ft 10in (28.60m)
Max Cruise: 495mph (797km/h)
Passengers: 112 plus two crew
First aircraft flown: 18 June 1991 (RJ70); 27 March 1992 (RJ85, the first Avro RJ prototype).
Production: 111 delivered by late 1998 with a further 39 on order.
Recent/current service: The first production RJ85 was delivered to Crossair in April 1993. Others include Air Malta, Delta Air Transport, Lufthansa CityLine, Pelita Air Services and Titan AW.
Recognition: Underwing-mounted engines in four nacelles. Slightly swept wings mounted on top of the fuselage, drooping towards the wingtips. Distinctive trailing-edge wing fillets. The fuselage is circular in section with bulges on the lower side to accommodate the undercarriage. The rectangular fin and rudder is slightly swept with a T-tailplane mounted on the top of the fin. There are sideways-opening airbrakes below the rudder.
Variants: The RJ70, RJ85 and RJ100 were introduced as replacements for the BAe 146-100, -200 and -300 respectively (see later). Principal changes include uprated engines and all-digital avionics. The RJ115 is a higher-capacity version of the RJ100, featuring six-abreast seating. There are freighter (Quiet Trader), convertible (Quick Change) and Combi versions of the RJ series. Avro is now considering another update for the RJ – the RJX, with reductions in weight, and different engines.

11

FOUR-ENGINED JET AIRLINERS

Boeing 707/720

Above:
Hushkits have been fitted to Boeing 707s to enable their continued operation. *PRM*

Four-turbofan medium/long-range transport

Basic data for Boeing 707-320B

Powerplant: Four Pratt & Whitney JT3D turbofans of 17,000lb st (75.7kN)
Span: 145ft 9in (44.42m)
Length: 152ft 11in (46.61m)
Max Cruise: 627mph (1,010km/h)
Passengers: 167 plus three/four crew
First aircraft flown: 15 July 1954 (707-80); January 1959 (707-300); 23 November 1959 (720).
Production: 1,009 Boeing 707s of which the main variants were the -320B and -320C (482 built); Boeing 720 (153 built). 124 Boeing 707s of all types were in non-military service in mid-1998, many for freighting or second-line operations.

Recent/current service: With Air Afrique, Air Atlantic Cargo, Air Memphis, Air Zimbabwe, Angola Air Charter, Beta Cargo, DAS Air, Egyptair, Iraqi AW, Kuwait AW, Libyan Arab AL, Middle East AL, Pakistan Int'l, Royal Jordanian AL, Saha AL, Sudan AW, TMA, Trans Arabian Air Transport and many others.
Recognition: Underwing-mounted engines in four separate pods. Swept narrow chord wing, low-set circular, narrow-body fuselage with the tailplane mounted either side of the tail cone. Tall, narrow fin and rudder, slightly swept, and a small ventral fin.
Variants: The various models of the 707/720 differ mainly in fuselage

length and powerplants. The original production 707-120 had a span of 130ft 10in (39.88m) and a length of 144ft 6in (44.04m); the -120B was re-engined with turbofans; the 707-320 was larger with a span of 142ft 5in (43.41m) and length of 152ft 11in (46.61m); the turbofan-engined -320B had a span of 145ft 9in (44.42m) with the 152ft 11in (46.61m) fuselage, while the -320C was similar but featured a large, port-side forward fuselage freight door. The 707-400 was a 707-300 with Rolls-Royce Conway 508s for service with BOAC, Air India, El Al, VARIG and Lufthansa. The 720 had the original short-span wings and a shorter fuselage of 136ft 2in (41.50m); the 720B was a turbofan-engined variant. Q707 – hush-kitted conversion by Contram. Burbank Aeronautical has developed a Stage 3 hushkit for the 707, and Omega Air is planning a P&W JT8D-200 re-engining programme. Under existing legislation, all 707s must be hushkitted at the turn of the century if they are to be operated into US or European airports.

FOUR-ENGINED JET AIRLINERS

Boeing 747-100, -200 and -300

Four-turbofan long-range airliner

Basic data for Boeing 747-200B

Above:
A cargo conversion of an early Boeing 747-100 series. PRM

Powerplant: Four General Electric CF6-50E2 turbofans of 52,500lb st (233.5kN); Rolls-Royce RB211-524D4-Bs of 50,000lb st (222.71kN); or Pratt & Whitney JT9D-7R4G2s of 54,750lb st (243.5kN)

Span: 195ft 8in (59.64m)

Length: 231ft 10in (70.70m)

Max Cruise: 610mph (981km/h)

Passengers: 365-480 plus three crew

First aircraft flown: 9 February 1969 (747-100); 1970 (747-200); 5 October 1982 (747-300).

Production: 205 747-100s of all versions, 384 747-200s of all versions and 81 747-300s were built.

Recent/current service: 173 747-100s, 361 747-200s and 79 747-300s in service late 1998. Operators include Aerolineas Argentinas, Air Canada, Air China, Air France, Air Hong Kong, Air-India, Air Pacific, Alitalia, All Nippon, British Airways, Air New Zealand, China AL, El Al, Evergreen, Garuda, Iberia, Iran Air, Japan AL, KLM, Korean Air, Lufthansa, Malaysia, Martinair, Northwest AL, Pakistan, Polar Air Cargo, Olympic, QANTAS, Saudia, South African AW, Swissair, TWA, United, UPS and Virgin Atlantic.

Recognition: Underwing-mounted engines in four separate nacelles. Swept, low-set wings which narrow towards the tips. Oval, wide-body fuselage with a distinctive short (but longer on the -300) raised fuselage forward of the wing, incorporating the cabin and flightdeck. Tall, swept fin with a fuselage-mounted tailplane below the rudder.

Variants: The Model 747-100 was the launch model, followed by the heavier -100B, an all-cargo -100F and the Combi -100C. The 747-200F is a freighter; 747-200 (SCD) a freighter with a side cargo door. The 747SR was a short-range version, based on the -100 for Japan Airlines. The 747-300 is essentially a Series 200 with a stretched upper deck.

Above:
Colourful Egyptair Boeing 747-366 in landing configuration. *PRM*

Below:
A Boeing 747-200 in El Al colours. *PRM*

Four-turbofan very long-range airliner

Basic data for Boeing 747-400

Above:
The Boeing 747-400 series has a longer fuselage, stretched upper deck, increased wingspan and 6ft-high winglets. PRM

Powerplant: Four Pratt & Whitney PW4056 turbofans of 56,750lb st (254kN); General Electric CF6-80C2B1Fs of 57,900lb st (251kN); or Rolls-Royce RB211-524Gs of 58,000lb st (258 kN), or RB211-524Hs of 60,000lb st (270kN)

Span: 211ft 5in (64.44m)

Length: 231ft 10in (70.70m)

Max Cruise: 583mph (938km/h)

Passengers: 421 plus two flight crew

First aircraft flown: 29 April 1988.

Production: The 747-400 is the only version marketed since May 1990. Over 433 delivered by late 1998 and over 148 on order.

Recent/current service: Includes Air Canada, Air China, Air France, Air-India, Air New Zealand, All Nippon, Asiana, British Airways, Cargolux, Cathay Pacific, China AL, El Al, Eva Air, Garuda, Japan AL, KLM, Korean Air, Lufthansa, Malaysian AL, Northwest AL, QANTAS, Saudia, Singapore AL, South African AW, Thai Int'l, United and Virgin Atlantic.

Recognition: Underwing-mounted engines in four separate nacelles. Swept, low-set wing with winglets, canted 22° outward and swept 60°. Upper deck extended rearwards by 23ft 4in (7.11m) compared with other versions. Tall swept fin with a fuselage-mounted tailplane below the rudder. The wing has a special aerofoil and 12ft 0in (3.66m) greater span than the 747-200.

Variants: The 747-400F combines the short upper deck of the -200F with the stronger and larger wing of the -400. The 747-400 Combi is a

passenger/freight version. Boeing is studying longer-range and stretched versions of the 747, known as the 747-500X and -600X respectively.

Above:
Japan Airlines operates this Boeing 747-400 series, with extra-stretched upper deck. *DJM*

Below:
Singapore Airlines Boeing 747-412 on approach to land. *DJM*

Boeing 747SP

Four-turbofan very long-range airliner

Above:
The very-short-fuselage Boeing 747SP of Korean Air. PRM

Basic data for Boeing 747SP (Special Performance)

Powerplant: Four Pratt & Whitney JT9D-7A turbofans of 46,950lb st (209kN) or JT9D-7Fs of 48,000lb st (218kN)
Span: 195ft 8in (59.64m)
Length: 184ft 9in (56.31m)
Max Cruise: 619mph (996km/h)
Passengers: 316 plus three crew
First aircraft flown: 4 July 1975.
Production: A total of 45 747SPs were built. Production ceased 1989.
Recent/current service: Air Atlanta Icelandic, Air China, Alliance AL, Corsair, Iran Air, Korean Air Lines, Mandarin AL, QANTAS, South African AW, Syrianair and United (ex-PanAm aircraft).

Recognition: Underwing-mounted engines in four separate nacelles. Swept, low-set wing which narrows towards the tip. Oval, wide-body fuselage – but much shorter (almost stubby), than other 747s – with a distinctive short raised fuselage forward of the wing, incorporating cabin and flightdeck. Tall swept fin with a fuselage-mounted tailplane below the rudder. Height of fin increased by 5ft 0in (1.52m) more than other 747s.
Variants: Six are currently flown by Royal/Government owners as 'biz jets'. Some have been heavily modified and fitted with a satellite communications dome behind the main 'hump'.

FOUR-ENGINED JET AIRLINERS

British Aerospace 146

Four-turbofan short/medium-range airliner

Basic data for BAe 146-300

Powerplant: Four Textron Lycoming ALF 502R-5 turbofans of 6,970lb st (31kN)
Span: 86ft 5in (26.34m)
Length: 101ft 8in (30.99m)
Max Cruise: 493mph (797km/h)
Passengers: 103 plus two crew (128 in high-density seating version)
First aircraft flown: 3 September 1981 (BAe 146-100); 1 August 1982 (146-200); 1 May 1987 (146-300).
Production: 219 were built and delivered. Production superseded by Avro International Aerospace's Avroliner range (Avro is a division of BAe Regional Aircraft) in 1993.
Recent/current service: 208 in service with Aer Lingus Commuter, Air China, Air Jet, AirLink, Air Wisconsin, Ansett Australia, Ansett New Zealand, British Regional AL, CityJet, China NW, Debonair, Delta Air Transport, Druk Air, Eurowings, Flightline, Hamburg AL, Jersey European AW, KLM uk, Meridiana, Pan Air, QANTAS Airlink, TNT/Air Foyle, Malmo Aviation, Manx AL,

QANTAS Airlink, Titan AW, Uni Air and WDL.
Recognition: Underwing-mounted engines in four nacelles. Slightly swept wings mounted on top of the fuselage, drooping towards the wingtips. Distinctive trailing edge wing fillets. The fuselage is circular in section with bulges on the lower side to accommodate the undercarriage. The rectangular fin and rudder is slightly swept with a T-tailplane mounted on top of the fin. There are sideways-opening airbrakes below the rudder.
Variants: Series 100, designed to operate from short or semi-prepared airstrips with minimal ground facilities – seating 82/94; Series 200, fuselage lengthened by 7ft 10in (2.39m) and seating 82/112; Series 300, development of Series 100 with increased length and seating 103/128. Statesman, executive version of all series. 146-QT Quiet Trader, freighter version of all series; 146/QC Convertible, convertible passenger/freight version of Series 200-QT and 300-QT. Early BAe 146s are being upgraded by British Aerospace Asset Management Jets (AMJ) particularly a cockpit upgrade with an AlliedSignal satellite-based GNS-XLS navigation system.

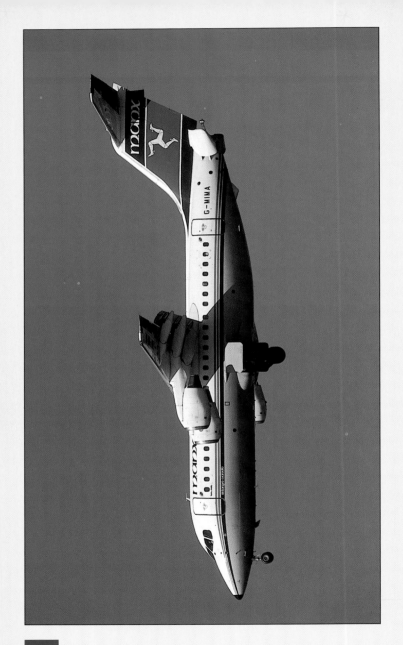

Four-turbofan long-range airliner

Basic data for Ilyushin Il-62MK

Powerplant: Four Soloviev D-30KU turbofans of 24,250lb st (107.9kN)
Span: 141ft 9in (43.20m)
Length: 174ft 3½in (53.12m)
Max Speed: 570mph (917km/h)
Passengers: 174 plus five crew
First aircraft flown: January 1963. Entered service in 1967.
Production: 285 built for Aeroflot and Soviet bloc airlines. Production ceased in 1994.
Recent/current service: Over 125 in service with 20 airlines including Aeroflot Russian Int'l AL, Air Koryo, Air Ukraine, Cubana, Domodedova AL, Far East Avia, Krasnoyarsk AL, Moscow AW, Rossia, Tarom and Uzbekistan AW.

Recognition: Rear fuselage side-mounted engines in two double nacelles. Swept wings, low-set on narrow body, circular fuselage. T-tailplane mounted on top of the swept fin and rudder. Distinctive bullet fairing projecting forward of the fin.

Variants: The internally improved Il-62MK has more powerful engines than the original Il-62. It carries more passengers but is externally identical.

Above:
The Ilyushin Il-62 has four rear-fuselage-mounted engines and a T-tail. *PRM*

Left:
One of many Il-62Ms operated by airlines in the CIS. *PRM*

FOUR-ENGINED JET AIRLINERS

Ilyushin Il-76

Left:
The 'military' glazed lower nose on this Aeroflot Il-76MA indicates dual military and airline use. *PRM*

Below:
Stretched Il-76MF, the forerunner of improved variants. *PRM*

Four-turbofan long-range transport

Basic data for Ilyushin Il-76T

Powerplant: Four Aviadvigatel D-30kp1 turbofans of 26,455lb st (118kN)
Span: 165ft 8in (50.50m)
Length: 152ft 10½in (46.60m)
Max Cruise: 497mph (800km/h)
Payload: 88,185lb or 90 passengers and five crew
First aircraft flown: 25 March 1971.
Production: Over 500 Il-76s built for civil airline use and at least 350 military Il-76M variants. In late 1998 320 were in airline service .
Recent/current service: With Aeroflot Russian Int'l AL, Air Koryo, Air Ukraine, Atlant, BSL, Domodedovo AL, HeavyLift Cargo AL, Ilavia, Inversija, Khors Air, Kras Air, Libyan Arab AL, Transavia Export, Turkmenistan AL, Tyumen AL, UHY, Ukrainian Cargo AW, Uzbekistan AW and Volare.
Recognition: Underwing-mounted engines in four nacelles. Slightly swept wings mounted on top of the fuselage, drooping towards the wingtips. Circular fuselage with large bulges on either side and below the lower fuselage section for the undercarriage. Rectangular swept fin and rudder on the raised rear fuselage, with the swept T-tailplane mounted on top of the fin. A bullet fairing projects forward from the junction of the fin and tailplane. The aircraft nose has distinctive windows in the lower half with a circular bulge behind.
Variants: The Il-76TD has internal cabin improvements and marginally better performance. The Il-76MD is a military version that appears in Aeroflot colours. Ilyushin has plans to re-engine the Il-76 with CFMI CFM56 turbofans and is actively replacing the DK-30s in 20 of the Russian airline's fleet with Perm PS-90A turbofans. The stretched (21ft 8in/6.6m) Il-76MF first flew in August 1995 and can seat up to 140 passengers. Powered by 35,232lb st (156.9kN) Aviadvigatel PS-90AN or 30,988lb st (138.8kN) CFM International CFM56 turbofans.

Four-turbofan medium-range airliner

Basic data for Ilyushin Il-86-300

Powerplant: Four Kuznetsov NK-86 turbofans of 28,660lb st (127kN)
Span: 157ft 8¼in (48.06m)
Length: 195ft 4in (59.54m)
Max Cruise: 590mph (949km/h)
Passengers: 350 plus three crew
First aircraft flown: 22 December 1976.
Production: 104 built by 1994 when production ceased.
Recent/current service: 95 were in airline service late 1998 with 14 airlines including Aeroflot Russian Int'l AL, Air Kazakhstan, Armenian AL, AJT Air, China Xinjiang AL, Eagle Airlines, Kras Air, Polkovo Aviation Enterprise, Sibir, Ural AL, Uzbekistan AW and Vnukovo AL.

Recognition: Underwing-mounted engines in four nacelles. Swept wings mounted on the lower section of the circular, wide-body fuselage. Swept fin and rudder with low-set swept tailplane mounted on the rear fuselage. Lower fuselage fairings beneath the wings.

Variants: The only variant was an engine change to the Soloviev PS90A introduced in 1990, though four military airborne command posts have been completed. There is a long-awaited project to re-engine the type with CFMI CFM56-5-C2 turbofans which now seems to have been delayed indefinitely because of funding problems.

Above:
Transaero is one of the main operators of the medium-range Il-86. *PRM*

Right:
Aeroflot operates the Il-86 on its high density routes. *Paul Gingell*

Four-turbofan long-range airliner

Basic data for Ilyushin Il-96-300

Powerplant: Four Aviadvigatel PS90A turbofans of 35,790lb st (159.2kN)
Span: 189ft 0in (57.60m)
Length: 181ft 7¼in (55.35m)
Max Speed: 552mph (888km/h)
Passengers: 300 plus crew of three
First aircraft flown: 28 September 1988.
Production: Production commenced 1993. Twelve ordered and 10 delivered by late 1998, while 20 Il-96Ms and Ts are on order for delivery from 1999.

Recent/current service: The Il-96-300 entered service with Aeroflot Russian Int'l AL (ARIA) on the Moscow-New York service on 14 July 1993. It is also in service with Domodedovo AL.
Recognition: Underwing-mounted engines in four separate pods. Swept narrow wings, with winglets, set low on circular wide-bodied fuselage. Tailplane mounted on either side of tail cone. Tall swept fin and rudder.
Variants: The Il-96M/MO is a stretched 375-seat version powered by Pratt & Whitney PW2337 engines of 164.6kN (36,960lb st), Smiths flight management system and western avionics. The Il-96T is a freight version of the -96M.

Above:
The Ilyushin Il-96T freighter has large winglets and large-diameter turbofan engines. *DJM*

Right:
A stretched fuselage and modified wings distinguish the Il-96M. *DJM*

Left:
A DC-8-71 long-fuselage freighter. *PRM*

Below:
DHL's DC-8-73AF freighter has the distinctive large-diameter CFM56 turbofans. *DJM*

Four-turbofan long-range transport

Basic data for DC-8 Series 60

Powerplant: Four Pratt & Whitney JT3D-1 turbofans of 17,000lb st (76kN)
Span: 142ft 5in (43.41m)
Length: 187ft 5in (57.1m)
Max Cruise: 595mph (958km/h)
Passengers: Maximum of 269 plus three crew
First aircraft flown: 30 May 1958 (DC-8-10); 20 November 1958 (DC-8-21); 21 February 1959 (DC-8-30); 20 December 1960 (DC-8-50).
Production: 556 of all variants, of which 263 remain in service, mostly being Super 60/70 series. 110 Super 70s were re-engined by Camacorp with CFM56-2-C5 engines.
Recent/current service: With some 42 airlines including Airborne Express, Air Transport Int'l, American Int'l AW, Arrow Air, DHL AW, Emery WW, Fine Air, Iberia, MK Airlines, Trans Continental AL and UPS (that has 49 freighters in service).

Recognition: Underwing-mounted engines in four pods. Swept wings mounted below the circular, narrow-body fuselage. Tall, slightly swept fin and rudder with a low swept tailplane mounted on the rear fuselage. Super 70 series has an extremely long fuselage.
Variants: The Series 10 through to 50 had differences of powerplant and performance but are externally all similar. The Series 55 had a large cargo door. Major changes came with the Super 60 series which had improved turbofan engines; the Series 61 had a considerably lengthened fuselage (36ft/11.18m longer); the Series 62 had a modest increase in length (6ft 8in/2.03m longer), extended wingtips making the span 148ft 5in (45.24m) and modified engine pods; the Series 63 has the longer fuselage (187ft 5in/57.12m total) and the extended wings of the Series 62. The re-engined Series 60 and 70 have CFM56-2-C5 turbofans which are shorter and of much greater diameter than the earlier powerplants. A Stage 3 hushkit has been developed by Burbank Aeronautical for the DC-8-62/63, which has been certified by the FAA. A Stage 3 kit is also being developed for the -50/-61. Another hushkit to receive certification is by Quiet Technology Venture (QTV).

Boeing 727

Three-turbofan medium-range airliner

Above:
American Airlines operates the Boeing 727-256 on its internal routes. *PRM*

Basic data for Boeing 727-200

Powerplant: Three Pratt & Whitney JT8D-17R turbofans of 15,500lb st (72kN)
Span: 108ft 0in (39.92m)
Length: 153ft 2in (46.69m)
Max Cruise: 599mph (964km/h)
Passengers: 189 plus three crew
First aircraft flown: 9 February 1963 (Series 100).
Production: A total of 1,831 built when production finished in August 1984, including 407 Series 100, 164 with large freight doors and 1,260 Series 200s and Advanced 200s.
Recent/current service: 1,445 were in service in late 1998 with approximately 100 operators worldwide including Air Algérie, American, Aviogenex, Comair, Continental, Delta, DHL, Emery Worldwide, European Air Transport, FedEx, Greyhound Air, Iberia, Iran Air, Iraqi AW, Istanbul AL, JAT, Kabo Air, Kelowna Flightcraft, Libyan Arab AL, Mexicana, Morning Star Air Express, Northwest, Olympic, Ryan Int'l, Sterling AW, Sun Country, Syrianair, Tunisair, TWA, United and UPS.
Recognition: Three rear-mounted engines, one on top of the fuselage at the base and forward of the fin, the other two in line either side of

THREE-ENGINED JET AIRLINERS
Boeing 727

Above:
Syrianair Boeing 727-294 *Palmyra.* DJM

the rear fuselage. Low-set swept wings midway along the circular narrow-body fuselage. Swept fin and rudder with T-tailplane.

Variants: The original 407 Series 100 was 10ft (3.05m) shorter than the Series 200 which was first flown on 27 July 1967 with more powerful engines and other improvements. Seventeen versions were built. The Advanced 200 has further power-plant and internal refinements. The first permanently re-engined Valsan 727-200s, with higher-bypass Pratt & Whitney JT8D-217Cs in acoustically treated nacelles are in service with launch customers Continental and Sterling Airways. FedEx has a large fleet of hushkitted 727-QFs specially adapted for freight use. Dee Howard is re-engining up to 80 727-100s with Rolls-Royce Tay 651-24 turbofans, marketed as the 727-100QF. The No 2 engine has a larger intake and S-duct. These companies offer modifications which reduce noise levels on the 727-200 below Stage 3 requirements without the need for a hushkit. Various conversion programmes are now being offered for re-engining and conversion to freighters.

27

Boeing (McDonnell Douglas) MD-11

Left:
An American Airlines long-range MD-11 shows its distinctive winglets. *PRM*

Below:
FedEx has a fleet of cargo MD-11s. *PRM*

Three-turbofan long-range airliner

Basic data for MD-11

Powerplant: Three General Electric CF6-80C2D1F turbofans of 61,500lb st (274kN) or Pratt & Whitney PW4460s of 60,000lb st (267kN)
Span: 169ft 10in (51.70m)
Length: 200ft 11in (61.24m)
Max Cruise: 578mph (930km/h)
Passengers: 250 to 405 maximum plus two crew
First aircraft flown: 10 January 1990.
Production: 180 delivered by late 1998, with orders for 16 outstanding.
Recent/current service: With 24 airlines including Aer Lingus, Alitalia, American, China Eastern, Delta, El Al, EVA Air, FedEx, Finnair, Japan AL, KLM, Korean Air, LTU, Lufthansa, Lufthansa Cargo, Mandarin AL, Martinair, Malaysian Air Service, Sabena, Saudi Arabian AL, Swissair, Thai AW, VARIG, VASP and World AW.

Recognition: Two engines in under-wing nacelles close to fuselage, one engine mounted on the fin above the fuselage with a straight-through exhaust pipe to the rear. A circular, wide-body fuselage with low-set, swept wings. Tailplane mid-set on the rear fuselage below the fin. Winglets are fitted.
Variants: The basic MD-11 has a DC-10 Srs 30 fuselage lengthened by 18ft 9in (5.71m). Combi and freighter variants are also in production. A series of longer range MD-11ERs, including a stretched version, was available from early 1996. Boeing, after its takeover of McDonnell Douglas, announced in June 1998 that assembly would be terminated in 2000, dashing hopes of continued output as a freighter.

Lockheed TriStar

Three-turbofan long-range airliner

Basic data for L-1011-1 TriStar

Powerplant: Three Rolls-Royce RB211-22B turbofans of 42,000lb st (187kN)

Span: 155ft 4in (47.35m)

Length: 177ft 10in (54.20m)

Max Cruise: 589mph (947km/h)

Passengers: 256-400 plus three crew

First aircraft flown: 16 November 1970.

Production: 249 built (including a development aircraft) by 1983 when production ceased. 185 still in service late 1998, and increasing numbers are being converted into freighters.

Recent/current service: 31 airlines worldwide use TriStars including Aer

Above:
Lockheed TriStar 500 in service with BWIA International. PRM

Lingus, Aer Turas, Air Lanka, Air Transat, American Trans Air, BWIA Int'l, Caledonia AW, Delta, Gulf Air, Novair, Peach Air, Royal Aviation, Royal Jordanian AL, Saudia, Star AL and TWA.

Recognition: Two engines in underwing nacelles and one engine mounted on top of the fuselage forward of the swept fin, with the jet efflux below the rudder through the tail cone. Circular wide-body fuselage with low-set swept wings at midway point. Swept tailplane low-set either side of the rear fuselage below the fin.

Variants: TriStar Series 1, 100 and 200 only have different versions of the RB211 turbofan and internal changes. The major variant is the

Lockheed TriStar

longer L-1011-500 (first flown 18 October 1978) which has extended wings to give a span of 164ft 4in (50.09m), 13ft 6in (4.12m) shorter fuselage (to 164ft 2in [50.04m]) and other internal modifications. The -500 can be recognised by its shorter fuselage, particularly forward of the wing, and in detail the reduction of port-side doors from four on the earlier models to three on this variant. The Lockheed 2000 is a dedicated all-freight conversion of the L-1011, featuring a large cargo door. Marshall Aerospace of Cambridge has developed a freighter variant of the TriStar.

Above:
A TriStar 500 operated by Delta from Atlanta. *DJM*

Below:
A Royal Jordanian TriStar. *PRM*

Three-turbofan long-range airliner

Basic data for DC-10-30

Above:
A DC-10 operated by the Indonesian carrier, Garuda. PRM

Powerplant: Three General Electric CF6-50C2 turbofans of 52,500lb st (234kN)
Span: 165ft 4in (50.42m)
Length: 182ft 1in (55.50m)
Max Cruise: 565mph (909km/h)
Passengers: 380 plus three crew
First aircraft flown: 29 August 1970.
Production: 386 by 1989 when production ceased (plus 60 KC-10s for the USAF). The MD-11 replaced the DC-10 in production. 339 still in airline service late 1998, plus 59 USAF KC-10s and two Dutch KDC-10s. Increasing numbers are being converted into freighters.
Recent/current service: With 44 airlines including American, AOM French AL, Biman Bangladesh, British Airways, Caledonian AL, Canadian, Condor, Continental, Continental Micronesia, DAS Air, FedEx, Garuda, Hawaiian, Japan AL, Laker, Monarch, Northwest, Premiair, Sun Country AL, Thai Int'l, Transaero, United, VARIG, VIASA and World AW.
Recognition: Two engines in under-wing nacelles close to the fuselage, one engine mounted on the fin above the fuselage with a straight-through exhaust pipe to the rear. A circular, wide-body fuselage with low-set, swept wings. Tailplane mid-set on the rear fuselage below the fin.
Variants: The initial two variants, DC-10-10 and -15, were externally identical; the -30 had a 10ft (3.05m) extension to the wing giving a span of 165ft 4in (50.39m) while the re-engined (Pratt & Whitney JT9D) -40

is slightly longer at 182ft 3in (55.55m). The only DC-10 variant more easily recognised is the combi/cargo (CF) version with a large port-side forward freight loading door. In 1995, MDC teamed with Alenia subsidiary Aeronavali to launch a product-improvement programme for the DC-10, aimed principally at the market for passenger-to-freight conversions.

Above:
A DC-10 of Continental Micronesia. *PRM*

Below:
AOM French Airlines DC-10-39 on take-off. *PRM*

Tupolev Tu-154

Left:
The tail-mounted engines and highly swept tailplane are evident on this Bulgarian Tu-154M.

Below:
Russian-designed Tupolev Tu-154B-2 operated by Malev, the Hungarian airline. *PRM*

Three-turbofan medium-range airliner

Basic data for Tupolev Tu-154M

Powerplant: Three Aviadvigatel D-30KU-154-II turbofans of 23,380lb st (104kN)
Span: 123ft 1¾in (37.55m)
Length: 157ft (47.90m)
Max Cruise: 590mph (950km/h)
Passengers: 168-180 plus three crew
First aircraft flown: 4 October 1968; 1983 (Tu-154M).
Production: Over 920 Tu-154s (A, B and M) built of which nearly 400 are Tu-154Ms, which variant remains in production. It is due to be replaced by the Tu-204.
Recent/current service: Over 580 in service with Aeroflot Russian Int'l AL and its many successor airlines; also operated by Akhal, Air Kazakhstan, Air Moldova, Air Ukraine, Armenian AL, Azerbaijan AL, Baikal AL, Balkan, Belavia, China NW, China SW, China United, CSA, Cubana, Donavia, Khabarovsk, Kish Air, KMV, Krasnoyarsk AL, Pulkovo, Sibir, Sichuan AL, Tarom, Tyumen, Ural and Uzbekistan AW.

Recognition: Two engines mounted either side of the rear fuselage with the third engine on top of the rear fuselage forward of the fin, exhausting through tail cone. Very swept wings set below the circular, narrow-body fuselage. Fairings for the undercarriage extend to the rear of the wings. A swept T-tailplane mounted on top of the fin and rudder with a bullet fairing projecting forward of the tailplane/fin intersection. The wings appear to droop towards the tips.

Variants: The three original versions operated in the West, the Tu-154, Tu-154A and Tu-154B, have no significant external differences, the main changes being in powerplant and internal improvements. The Tu-154M has a modified tailplane and spoilers. A cargo conversion, the Tu-154S, has a large port-side forward freight door.

Yakovlev Yak-42

Three-turbofan short/medium-range airliner

Above:
A Yak-42D operated by Air Moldova International.
PRM

Basic data for Yak-42D

Powerplant: Three Lotarev D-36 turbofans of 14,300lb st (63.7kN)
Span: 114ft 5¼in (34.88m)
Length: 119ft 4¼in (36.38m)
Max Cruise: 503mph (810km/h)
Passengers: 120 plus two crew
First aircraft flown: 7 March 1975.
Production: About 176 have been built by late 1998.
Recent/current service: 149 in service with 38 airlines including Aeroflot Russian Int'l AL, Air Ukraine, Bykovo Avia, China General, Cubana, Iran Air Tours, Karat, Kuban, Lithuanian AL, Saravia Saratov, Tatarstan Kazan, Turkmenistan AL and Volga AL.
Recognition: Two engines mounted either side of the rear fuselage with the third engine on top of the rear fuselage forward of the fin, exhausting through tail cone. Swept wing set low on the circular, narrow, short fuselage. Swept fin and rudder and swept T-tailplane set at the top of the fin.
Variants: The Yak-42 was the basic standard model. The Yak-42D is the increased range version with 120 passengers and remains in production. The Yak-142 is a partly westernised version of the Yak-42D, with upgraded AlliedSignal avionics, but retaining the D-36 turbofans. The Yak-242 has two underwing Aviadvigatel PS-90A12 turbofans, with passenger capacity of 130-180, and flew in 1995. The Yak-46 is a proposed development of the Yak-242 with Progress D-727 high-bypass turbofans but not likely to fly until 2000.

Left:
An Airbus A300B4 flown by Olympic Airways. *DJM*

Below:
China Southern is one of many Asian airlines operating the Airbus A300. *PRM*

Twin-turbofan medium/long-range airliner

Basic data for Airbus A300-600R

Powerplant: Two General Electric CF6-80C2A5 turbofans of 61,600lb st (273.6kN) or Pratt & Whitney PW4158s of 58,000lb st (258kN)
Span: 147ft 1in (44.84m)
Length: 177ft 5in (54.08m)
Max Cruise: 557mph (897km/h)
Passengers: 360 plus two crew
First aircraft flown: 28 October 1972 (A300B); 8 July 1983 (A300-600).
Production: Over 481 delivered by December 1998 with a further 39 on order. The current production model is the -600R.
Recent/current service: With 54 airlines worldwide, including Air Afrique, Air Alfa, Air France, Air-India, Alitalia, American, Carnival AL, China AL, China Eastern, China Northern, China NW, Egyptair, Emirates, European Air Transport, FedEx, Garuda, HeavyLift Cargo AL, Iberia, Indian, Iran Air, Japan Air System, Korean Air, Kuwait AW, Lufthansa, Monarch, Olympic, Pakistan Int'l, PanAm World AW, Premiair, Qatar AW, Saudia, South African AW and Thai Int'l.

Recognition: Engines are carried in nacelles under and projecting forward of the wings. Circular wide-body fuselage, tapering towards the tail. Low-set, swept wings with five underwing fences/flap fairings. Tall, swept fin and rudder and a swept tailplane set either side of the rear fuselage cone below the rudder.

Variants: Differ mainly in power-plants and internal refinements. The A300C4 features a large fuselage side-loading door. First major difference comes with the extended range A300B4-600 which has a modified (A310 style) rear fuselage with a longer parallel section and more sharply tapered tail cone. The 600R has tailplane fuel tanks for increased range (180min ETOPS). The A300-600 convertible is a passenger/cargo version.

Airbus A300 Freighter

Left:
Airbus A300 Freighter converted from a passenger aircraft to a freighter by British Aerospace Aviation Services. PRM

Below:
DHL is building up a fleet of A300Fs for its extensive parcel service. PRM

Twin-turbofan medium/long-range freighter

Basic data for Airbus A300F

Powerplant: Two General Electric CF6-80C2A5 turbofans of 61,600lb st (273.6kN) or Pratt & Whitney PW4158s of 58,000lb st (258kN)
Span: 147ft 1in (44.84m)
Length: 177ft 5in (54.08m)
Max Cruise: 557mph (897km/h)
Passengers: None, two crew only
First aircraft flown: Most freighters are conversions of existing A300 airliners, but some are new-build aircraft (for City Bird). The first conversion (ordered by Channel Express) flew on 23 January 1997.
Recent/current service: With C-S Aviation Services (CAS), the major lease management provider of freight aircraft with 28 in its fleet, Channel Express, DHL, Egyptair and JHM Cargo Express. Conversion orders are in excess of 45. UPS announced a major purchase for 30 A300-600 Freighters in late 1998, the first to be delivered in 2000.
Recognition: Engines are carried in nacelles under and projecting forward of the wings. Circular wide-body windowless fuselage, tapering towards tail. Cargo doors inserted in fuselage. Low-set, swept wings with five underwing fences/flap fairings. Tall, swept fin and rudder and a swept tailplane.
Variants: Conversions are undertaken by British Aerospace Aviation Services (BAe AS) at Filton, Bristol and Daimler-Benz Aerospace (DASA) Airbus at Hamburg in Germany. The pure freighter has a capacious cargo door and reinforced floor.

Above:
An Airbus A310 of Swissair, an early operator of the airliner. PRM

Twin-turbofan medium/extended-range airliner

Basic data for Airbus A310-300

Powerplant: Two General Electric CF6-80C2A8 turbofans of 59,000lb st (262.4kN) or Pratt & Whitney PW4156As of 56,000lb st (249.1kN)
Span: 144ft 0in (43.89m)
Length: 153ft 1in (46.66m)
Max Cruise: 556mph (895km/h)
Passengers: 280 plus two crew
First aircraft flown: 3 April 1982.
Production: Total of 255 A310s delivered by late 1998.
Recent/current service: In service with 44 airlines including Aeroflot Russian Int'l AL, Aerolineas Argentinas, Air Algérie, Air France, Air-India, Air Jamaica, Austrian AL, Biman Bangladesh, China NW AL, CSA, Cyprus AW, Emirates, FedEx, Hapag-Lloyd, Kenya AW, Kuwait AW, Lufthansa, Merpati Nusantara, Middle East AL, Nigeria AW, Pakistan, Royal Aviation, Royal Jordanian AL, Singapore AL, Swissair, TAP Air Portugal, Tarom, Thai, THY, Uzbekistan AW and Yemenia.
Recognition: Underwing-mounted engines in nacelles projecting forward of the wings. Circular wide-body fuselage tapering upwards towards the tail. Low-set, swept wings with four underwing fences/fairings. Tall, swept fin and rudder and a swept tailplane set either side of the rear fuselage cone below the rudder. The A310 is 22ft 10in (6.96m) shorter than the A300

*THAI

TWIN-ENGINED JET AIRLINERS
Airbus A310

and has a new wing of shorter span, but retains the same fuselage cross-section as the A300.
Variants: The A310-200 and -220 differ in powerplants while the -300, the extended range version, features winglets and interior refinements. Convertible (-200C) and freighter (-200F) versions have a side freight

Above:
An Aeroflot Airbus A310-203. *PRM*

Below:
A Royal Jordanian Airbus A310-304. *DJM*

door. Airbus is studying the A310 follow-on project under the development name P305.

Left:
An Airbus A320 Series 200 used by British Airways on its European services.

Below:
One of many A320s in service with Asian airlines. *PRM*

Twin-turbofan medium-range airliner

Basic data for Airbus A320-200

Powerplant: Two CFMI CFM56-5B4 turbofans of 27,400lb st (122kN); IAE V2500-A1, IAE V2527-A5 or CFM56-5B4 alternatives
Span: 111ft 10in (34.10m)
Length: 123ft 3in (37.57m)
Max Cruise: 561mph (903km/h)
Passengers: 180 maximum plus two crew
First aircraft flown: 22 February 1987.
Production: By end of 1998 a total of 691 A320s had been delivered with a further 413 on order.
Recent/current service: With 70 airlines including Adria, Aero Lloyd, Air 2000, Air Canada, Air France, Air Lanka, Air Malta, Airtours, All Nippon AW, America West, Ansett Australia, British Airways, British Mediterranean AW, Caledonian AW, Canada 3000, Canadian Int'l AL, China Eastern, China NW, China Southern, Cyprus AW, Dragonair, Egypt Air, Eurocypria, Flying Colours/Airworld, Gulf Air, Iberia, Indian Airlines, Kuwait AW, Leisure International, Lotus Air, Lufthansa, Mexicana, Middle East AL, Monarch, Northwest AL, Premiair, Royal Jordanian AL, Sichuan AL, South African AW, Swissair, Syrianair, TAP Air Portugal, THY, Transasia, Tunis Air, United AL, Vietnam AL, Virgin Atlantic and Virgin Express.

Recognition: Underwing-mounted engines in nacelles protruding forward of the wings. Circular narrow-body fuselage tapering upwards towards the tail. Low-set, swept wings of narrow chord with three trailing-edge fairings and winglets. Tall, swept fin and rudder set forward of tail cone. Swept tailplane with dihedral.

Variants: The A320-100 is the 130/140-seat version, only 21 of which were built.

Airbus A318/319/A321

Twin-turbofan medium-range airliner

Above:
The Airbus A321-112 entered service with Alitalia in 1994. DJM

Basic data for Airbus A321-100

Powerplant: Two CFM International CFM56-5B1 turbofans of 30,000lb st (133.4kN) or IAE V2530-A5s of 30,500lb st (133.5kN)
Span: 111ft 10in (34.1m)
Length: 146ft 0in (44.51m)
Max Cruise: 560mph (890km/h)
Passengers: A321 – 176-220 plus two crew; A319 – 130 plus two crew
First aircraft flown: 25 August 1995 (A319); 11 March 1993 (A321).
Production: A319 – 118 delivered and 436 on order; A321 – 111 delivered and 141 on order in late 1998.
Recent/current service: Launch customers of the A321 were Lufthansa and Alitalia in 1994. Also in service with Air Canada, Air France, Aer Lingus, Air Macu, Austrian AL, Egyptair, Finnair, Flying Colours/Airworld, Middle East AL, Monarch, Onur Air, Sichuan AL, Swissair, TAP Air Portugal and Transasia. Launch customers of the A319 were Air France, Lufthansa and Swissair in 1996, followed by Air Canada, America West, Eurowings, Finnair, Swissair, TAP Air Portugal, United and US Airways.
Recognition: Underwing-mounted engines in nacelles protruding forward. Circular narrow-body fuselage (6.93m longer on the A321 than the A320; 3.73m shorter on the long-range A319 than the A320) tapering upwards towards the tail. Low-set, swept wings of narrow chord with three trailing-edge fairings and winglets. Emergency exits repositioned to either side of the wing leading- and trailing-edges.

Above:
The Airbus A321 has a 22.75ft stretched fuselage.

Below:
The Airbus A319's fuselage is noticeably shorter. *DJM*

Variants: The A319 is 12ft 4in (3.73m) shorter than the A320. Growth versions available at higher weights. A321-100 is 22ft 9in (6.93m) longer than the A320. A321-200 has increased weight plus more powerful engines and increased fuel. The Airbus A318 will enter the 100-seat market in 2002, powered by the P&W 6000. It will be 4.5 frames shorter than the A319.

TWIN-ENGINED JET AIRLINERS

Airbus A330

Twin-turbofan long-range airliner

Basic data for Airbus A330-300

Powerplant: Two General Electric CF6-80E1 turbofans of 71,000lb st (317kN); Rolls-Royce Trent 768/772s of 72,000lb st (322kN); or Pratt & Whitney PW4164/4168s of 69,000lb st (308kN)

Span: 197ft 8in (60.30m)

Length: 208ft 10in (63.65m)

Max Cruise: 575mph (925km/h)

Passengers: Up to 440 plus two crew

First aircraft flown: 2 November 1992.

Production: 87 delivered by late 1998 and a further 161 on order.

Recent/current service: Entered service in 1994 with Aer Lingus and Thai Air Int'l. Also in service with Air France, Cathay Pacific, Corsair,

Above:
The Airbus A330 entered service with Cathay Pacific Airways in 1995. PRM

Dragonair, Emirates, Garuda Indonesia, Korean Air, LTU, Malaysia AL, Sabena, Swissair and TAM.

Recognition: Two large underwing-mounted engines in nacelles protruding forward of the wings. Long circular narrow-body fuselage tapering upwards to the tail. Low-set wings of narrow chord with winglets and four trailing-edge fairings. Tall, swept fin and rudder set forward of tail cone. Swept tailplane with dihedral. Identical to A340 but with two engines.

Variants: Engine options with the first Rolls-Royce Trent-powered A330s entered service with Cathay Pacific early in 1995. A higher gross weight version was available from 1996. A shortened A330-200 was launched in the same year which seats 256 passengers.

Below:
Aer Lingus replaced its Boeing 747s on the North Atlantic route with the Airbus A330. *PRM*

Left:
With overwing protruding engines, the An-72 has a distinctive appearance. *PRM*

Below:
A high-set tailplane and tapered wing are notable features of the An-72. *PRM*

Twin-turbofan regional airliner/STOL utility transport

Basic data for An-72A

Powerplant: Two ZMKB Progress D-36 turbofans of 14,300lb st (63.7kN)
Span: 104ft 8in (31.89m)
Length: 92ft 1in (28.07m)
Max Cruise: 373mph (600km/h)
Passengers: 52 plus two/three crew
First aircraft flown: 22 December 1977.
Production: Over 150 delivered, including military versions.
Recent/current service: 30 An-72s and 25 An-74s in airline service as at late 1998, mainly in Eastern Europe.
Recognition: High, swept wing with large high-bypass turbofan intakes mounted over-wing, to produce the Coanda effect to improve STOL performance – this uses engine exhaust gases blown over the wing's upper surface to boost lift. Multi-slatted flaps. Rear-loading ramp. Large, swept tail surfaces. Four large main-wheels, mounted in tandem, for operations from unprepared strips, or from surfaces covered with ice or snow. Provision for combined wheel/ski landing gear.
Variants: An-72S is a VIP transport. The An-72P is a maritime patrol version, the An-74T/TK the freighter/combi derivative. Only produced for civil use thus far, the An-74 is optimised for all-weather operations, including Arctic missions, and was intended as a STOL jet successor in this role for the An-26.

Above:
A Boeing 717-200 at Long Beach, California.
BOEING

Twin-turbofan short/medium-range airliner

Basic data for Boeing 717-210

Powerplant: Two BMW/Rolls-Royce BR715-58 turbofans of 21,983lb st (97.9kN)
Span: 93ft 2in (28.4m)
Length: 124ft 0in (37.8m)
Max Cruise: 503mph (810km/h)
Passengers: 106 plus two crew
First aircraft flown: 2 September 1998.
Production: Orders for 55 as of late 1998. First deliveries are scheduled for AirTran (previously ValuJet) and Bavaria Leasing in mid-1999.
Recent/current service: AirTran Airlines is the launch customer, which will take the first of 50 on order in mid-1999.

Recognition: Effectively a new-generation development of the DC-9 twinjet. Low-set, swept wings which taper towards the tips with non-swept inboard trailing-edges. Engines mounted on the sides of the rear fuselage forward of the swept fin and rudder.

Variants: The 717-200 can be configured with 106-130 seats, while the 717-200(HGW) is the higher gross-weight version (the type was previously known as the MD-95-30ER). Boeing is studying smaller and larger derivatives to extend the 717 family, ranging from the 75/80-seat -100X to the 130-seat -300X proposal.

Boeing 737-100/200

Twin-turbofan medium-range airliner

Basic data for Boeing 737-200

Powerplant: Two Pratt & Whitney JT8D-15A turbofans of 16,000lb st (71kN)

Span: 93ft 0in (28.35m)

Length: 100ft 2in (30.53m)

Max Cruise: 560mph (903km/h)

Passengers: 130 plus two crew

First aircraft flown: 9 April 1967.

Production: 1,144 'pre-300' series completed when production ceased August 1988.

Recent/current service: Over 940 remain in service with 175 airlines worldwide including Aerolineas Argentinas, Air Algérie, Air France, Air Malta, Air New Zealand, Air Toulouse, All Nippon, Aloha, American West, Bouraq Indonesian, British Airways, Canadian AL, Continental, Croatia AL, Delta, GB Airways, Indian AL, Japan Transocean, LAN Chile, Lithuanian AL, Lufthansa, Malev, Mandala AL, Nigerian, Olympic, Ryanair, Sabena, Saudia, South African Airways, Southwest AL, TAP Air Portugal, TAT, Transaero, United, US Airways, VARIG, VASP, Virgin Express and WestJet AL.

Recognition: Slim engines mounted directly under the swept wings and projecting in front and behind. Tubby, circular fuselage with wings set in the lower section. Tall, angular, slightly swept fin and rudder with the swept tailplane set on the rear fuselage at the base of the rudder.

Variants: Series 100 had a 6ft (1.83m) shorter fuselage, but only 30 built before the larger Series 200 entered production. The -200C has a large freight door on the port side of the forward fuselage. Hushkits for the type's P&W JT8D engines are offered by Nordam and AvAero.

Above:
A second-generation Boeing 737-300 series powered by CFM56 turbofans. *PRM*

Twin-turbofan medium-range airliner

Basic data for Boeing 737-300

Powerplant: Two CFM56-3C-1 turbofans of 22,000lb st (98kN)
Span: 94ft 9in (28.88m)
Length: 109ft 7in (33.40m)
Max Cruise: 564mph (908km/h)
Passengers: Up to 149 plus two crew
First aircraft flown: 24 February 1984 (-300), 19 February 1988 (-400), 20 June 1989 (-500).
Production: 1,765 delivered by late 1998 with further orders standing at over 170.
Recent/current service: With more than 120 airlines worldwide, including AB Airlines, Aeroflot, Air China, Air Europa, Air France, Air Holland, Air Malta, Air New Zealand, Air Pacific, American West, Ansett Australia, Asiana, Braathens, British Airways, British Midland, China Southern, China SW, Condor, Continental, Debonair, Delta, Deutsche-BA, easyJet, GB Airways, Germania, Go, Icelandair, KLM, Lauda Air, LOT, Lufthansa, Luxair, Maersk Air, Malaysia, Malev, Olympic, QANTAS, Royal Air Maroc, Sabena, Silk Air, Southwest AL, TAP Air Portugal, Tarom, Thai, THY, Transbrasil, Transavia, United, US Airways, VARIG, Virgin Express, Viva Air and Western Pacific.

Recognition: Large engines, with oval nacelles, noticeably flat at bottom to increase ground clearance, mounted under and forward of the swept wings. Circular fuselage with wings set in the lower section. Tall, angular, slightly swept fin and rudder with a pronounced dorsal fin. Swept tailplane set on the rear fuselage at the base of the rudder.

Variants: 737-400 series is 10ft (3m) longer than the -300 accommodating 168 passengers in its 119ft 7in (36.4m) fuselage, and powered by two CFM56-3C turbofans of 23,500lb st (104.5kN). The -500 series has the short fuselage of the 200, with two CFM56-3-B1 turbofans of 20,000lb st (89kN). It carries up to 132 passengers in the all-economy version, or 108 in mixed-class configuration. First delivery was February 1990 to Southwest Airlines. With the introduction of the next-generation 737 family in 1998, the earlier CFM56-powered models are now commonly referred to as the 'Classic'.

Above:
The shorter fuselage Boeing 737-500 of Balkan Bulgarian Airlines.
PRM

Left:
A Boeing 737-400 Series operated by British Midland. *DJM*

Twin-turbofan medium-range airliner

Above:
The first of three Next-Generation 737-800's delivered to Air Europa takes to the skies. BOEING

Basic data for Boeing 737-600

Powerplant: Two CFM International CFM56-7B-18 turbofans of 22,000lb st (82kN)
Span: 112ft 6in (34.32m)
Length: 102ft 6in (31.24m)
Max Cruise: 588mph (946km/h)
Passengers: 132 (plus two crew)
Production: The 737-600 is to replace the -500; the 737-700, the -300; and the 737-800, the -400. Over 940 are on order, and 53 have been delivered, by late 1998.
Recent/current service: The 737-600 was launched following an order from Scandinavian Airlines System for 49 aircraft, entering service on 18 September 1998. The -700 entered service with Southwest AL in October 1997, and Air Pacific in 1998 and COPA in 1999. China Airlines became the initial -800 user in October 1998, followed by THY, Hapag Lloyd, Euralair and American AL, Sterling European.
Recognition: The 737-600/-700/-800 are longer than the -500/-300/-400 that they replace. Differences include increased wing chord and span, wing area being increased by 25% and increased height and area of the vertical fin and the span and area of the horizontal stabiliser.
Variants: These 737-600/-700/-800 variants complete the latest revamp of the 737 family. A dedicated Business Jet version has been developed, which incorporates the -700's fuselage with the engines and strengthened wing of the -800. The 737-900 is due to fly in 2000, with its launch customer, Alaska, taking delivery a year later.

TWIN-ENGINED JET AIRLINERS
Boeing 757

Left:
Slender lines of a Boeing 757-225ER operated by Air 2000. *DJM*

Below:
Boeing 757s have distinctly long, narrow fuselages. *DJM*

Twin-turbofan short/medium/extended-range airliner

Basic data for Boeing 757-200

Powerplant: Two Rolls-Royce RB211-535E4 turbofans of 40,100lb st (178kN) or Pratt & Whitney PW2040s of 41,542lb st (185kN)
Span: 124ft 10in (38.05m)
Length: 155ft 3in (47.32m)
Max Cruise: 569mph (916km/h)
Passengers: Maximum of 235 plus two crew
First aircraft flown: 19 February 1982; 11 August 1987 (757-200PF).
Production: 807 delivered by late 1998, with 115 on order.
Recent/current service: With 58 airlines including Aeromexico, Air 2000, Air Europa, Air Holland, Airtours Int'l, American, America West AL, Britannia, British Airways, Canada 3000 AL, China Southern, China South West, Condor Flug, Continental, Delta, El Al, Ethiopian AL, Far Eastern Air Transport, Iberia, Icelandair, LTU-Sud, Malev, Monarch, Northwest, Royal Air Maroc, Shanghai AL, Transaero, Transavia, Transbrasil, Transworld, TWA, United, UPS and US Airways.

Recognition: Engines in nacelles under the wings. A very long, circular, narrow-body fuselage with swept, low-set wings at the midway point, giving the appearance of a very long nose. A pronounced lower fuselage bulge for the undercarriage fairing. A tall, swept fin and rudder with a swept tailplane on either side of the rear fuselage below the fin.

Variants: The Boeing 757-200PF freighter has a forward cargo door and a windowless fuselage. The 757-200M Combi has forward port cargo door and carries up to 150 passengers. The 757-200ER is the extended range version. The 757-300, which is 7.1m longer, was first flown on 2 August 1998.

Twin-turbofan medium/long-range airliner

Above:
Boeing 767-338ER of QANTAS, showing the much deeper fuselage of the 767 compared to the 757.
PRM

Basic data for Boeing 767-300ER

Powerplant: Two General Electric CF6-80C2B6F turbofans of 56,475lb st (251kN) or Pratt & Whitney PW4060s of 60,300lb st (268kN)
Span: 156ft 1in (47.57m)
Length: 180ft 3in (54.94m)
Max Cruise: 565mph (910km/h)
Passengers: Maximum of 328 plus two crew
First aircraft flown: 26 September 1981 (767-200); 30 January 1986 (767-300).
Production: 706 delivered by late 1998 with 122 on order.
Recent/current service: Over 70 airlines fly 767s including Aeroflot Russian Int'l AL, Air Algérie, Air Canada, Air China, Air Europe, Air France, Air New Zealand, Airborne Express, Airtours Int'l, Alitalia, American Airlines, Ansett Australia, Asiana, All Nippon, Balkan Bulgarian AL, British Airways, Britannia, Canadian AL Int'l, City Bird, Condor Flug, Delta, Egyptair, El Al, Ethiopian, Eurofly, EVA Air, Gulf Air, Japan AL, KLM, LAN Chile, Lauda Air, Leisure Int'l, LOT, LTU, Malev, Martinair, QANTAS, Royal Brunei, SAS, Spanair, TransBrasil, TWA, United, US Airways, VARIG and Vietnam AL.

TWIN-ENGINED JET AIRLINERS
Boeing 767

Left:
Shorter fuselage of the Series 200ER Boeing 767. *PRM*

Below:
A Boeing 767-383ER (Extended Range) of Scandinavian Airlines. *PRM*

Recognition: Turbofans mounted under the swept wings. Circular fuselage (bulkier than the 757) with the wings set in the lower section, midway between the nose and tail. Very tall swept fin with the tailplane set on the rear fuselage at the base of the rudder.

Variants: The original 767-200 200/210-seat version had a length of 159ft 2in (48.51m). British Airways was the launch customer (11) for a Rolls-Royce RB-211-535-engined version of the 767-300ER (extended range). The 767-300F freighter entered service with launch customer UPS in October 1995. It has a large forward port side freight door but no cabin windows. Timco is modifying a fleet of ex-All Nippon 767-200s, but with no cargo doors. In 1997, Boeing launched a further stretched version, the -400ER, with an upgraded flightdeck based on the 777. It is also projecting the 767-400X development (the second stretch) with a larger, redesigned wing including winglets, more powerful engines and other refinements to fly faster over a greater range (9,600km) and with a higher payload (25% more cargo or 10% lower seat/km costs).

Left:
The Boeing 777 entered service with Emirates Airlines in 1996. *PRM*

Below:
The triple-bogie wheels are evident on this United Airlines Boeing 777. *PRM*

Twin-turbofan long-range high-capacity airliner

Basic data for Boeing 777-200ER

Powerplant: Two General Electric GE90-85B turbofans of 84,700lb st (377kN) or Pratt & Whitney PW4077s of 76,950lb st (342kN)
Span: 199ft 11in (61.00m)
Length: 209ft 1in (63.73m)
Max Cruise: 572mph (923km/h)
Passengers: 440 plus two crew
First aircraft flown: 12 June 1994.
Production: 141 delivered by late 1998 with 251 on order.
Recent/current service: Entered service with United in June 1995 and British Airways in November 1995. Also flown by Aeroflot Russian Int'l AL, All Nippon AL, Cathay Pacific, China Southern AL, Continental, Emirates, Japan AL, Japan Air System, Korean Air, Kuwait AW, Lauda Air, Malaysian, Saudia, Singapore AL and Thai Int'l.
Recognition: The world's largest twin-jet. Six mainwheels on each bogie. New wing of 31.6° sweep-back. Cylindrical fuselage wider than 767. Outer wings fold to vertical to reduce gate width requirement at airports. Very tall swept fin with the tailplane set on the rear fuselage at the base of the rudder.
Variants: The 200 IGW (increased gross-weight version) with longer range entered service with BA in September 1996. The 300 series was announced at the 1995 Paris Salon; it is capable of seating 420 passengers in a three-class layout, and is 3m longer than the 747. Engines to include 400kN Rolls-Royce Trent 8104 turbofans as an option. The next developments are the very long-range -200X and -300X.

Boeing (McDonnell Douglas) MD-80 Series

Twin-turbofan short/medium-range airliner

Above:
This MD-82 of Reno Air has more powerful engines. PRM

Basic data for MD-81

Powerplant: Two Pratt & Whitney JT8D-209 turbofans of 19,250lb st (85.6kN)
Span: 107ft 10in (32.87m)
Length: 147ft 11in (45.08m)
Max Cruise: 574mph (924km/h)
Passengers: Maximum 172 plus two crew
First aircraft flown: 18 October 1979 (MD-80); 17 December 1984 (MD-83); 4 December 1986 (MD-87).
Production: Total of 1,160 MD-80 variants in airline service in late 1998, though the type is due to be phased out by 2000.
Recent/current service: In the inventories of 55 airlines including Aero Lloyd, AeroMexico, Air Liberté, AirTran, Alaska, Alitalia, American, AOM French AL, Austrian, Aviaco, Avianca, BWIA Int'l, China Eastern, China Northern, Continental, Crossair, Delta, Eurofly, Finnair, Iberia, Japan Air System, Korean Air, Meridiana, Northwest, Nouvelair Tunisie, Onur Air, Reno Air, SAS, Spanair, Sun Air, TWA and US Airways.

Recognition: Engines mounted on the sides of the rear fuselage forward of the swept fin and rudder that is 10in taller than the DC-9's. Low-set swept wings which taper towards the tips with non-swept

inboard trailing-edges. Narrow-body, circular fuselage considerably extended forward of the wings compared with the earlier DC-9 series.

Above:
This MD-81 development of the DC-9 has a stretched fuselage. DJM

Below:
Shorter-fuselage MD-87 operated by Iberia. PRM

Variants: Originally known as the Super 80, the MD-80 series has the following sub-types:

MD-81 as above;

MD-82 'hot-and-high' version with more powerful JT8D-217 turbofans of 20,850lb st (93kN);

MD-83 extended range version with JT8D-219s of 21,650lb st (96.5kN);

MD-87 shorter fuselage length 130ft 6in (39.73m), JT8D-217 turbofans and carries 139 single-class passengers;

MD-88 longer fuselage length 147ft 11in (45.08m) and JT8D-217 turbofans, carrying 172 passengers.

A small number of MD-80s has been assembled from kits in Shanghai, China.

Twin-turbofan short/medium-range airliner

Basic data for MD-90-30

Above:
The improved MD-90 entered service in 1995. *PRM*

Below:
China Southern was an early customer for the stretched MD-90. *PRM*

Powerplant: Two IAE V2500-D1 or V2528-D5 turbofans of 24,973lb st (111.21kN)
Span: 107ft 9½in (32.86m)
Length: 152ft ½in (46.50m)
Max Cruise: 504mph (811km/h)
Passengers: 172 plus two crew
First aircraft flown: August 1993.
Production: 78 delivered by late 1998 with approximately 90 others on order.
Recent/current service: The first MD-90-30 entered service with Delta Air Lines in 1995. Also in service with ASERCA, China Northern AL, Eva Air, Great China AL, Japan Air System, Reno Air and SAS.
Recognition: A follow-on to the MD-80 series. The MD-90-30 fuselage is

lengthened by 4ft 9in (1.45m). Low-set swept wings which taper towards the tips with non-swept inboard trailing-edges. Engines mounted on the sides of the rear fuselage forward of the swept fin and rudder.
Variants: The MD-90-50 extended range version with 28,000lb st (124.7kN) IAE V2528-D5 turbofans. MD-90-55 similar to -50 but with extra doors in forward fuselage to allow maximum of 203 passengers. MD-90-30T Trunkliner version – 40 being built in China.

Left:
The Bombardier Canadair Regional Jet features winglets and five small underwing flap fairings. *PRM*

Below:
A Bombardier Canadair CL-600-2B19 Regional Jet of Lufthansa City Line. *PRM*

Twin-turbofan regional airliner

Basic data for Bombardier Canadair Regional Jet Series 100

Powerplant: Two General Electric CF34-34A1 or CF34-3B1 turbofans of 9,200lb st (41kN)
Span: 69ft 7in (21.21m)
Length: 87ft 10in (26.77m)
Max Cruise: 529mph (851km/h)
Passengers: 50 plus two crew
First aircraft flown: 10 May 1991.
Production: After an initial delivery of three to Lauda Air, 240 more had been delivered to 17 airlines by late 1998, with a further 135 on order.
Recent/current service: With Air Canada, AMR Eagle, Atlantic Coast AL, Atlantic SE, Brit Air, Campagne Air Littoral, China United, Comair, Dac Air, Lauda Air, Lufthansa CityLine, Mesa, Midway, Skywest AL, Southern Winds and Tyrolean AW.

Recognition: Based on the Challenger business jet which it strongly resembles. Twin engines mounted on the sides of the rear fuselage forward of tail. Low-set wings in the lower section of the circular fuselage. Swept fin with a square top and a swept tailplane set at the top of the fin with very small dorsal fillet (for APU). Swept tapered wings, with winglets and five small underwing flap fairings.

Variants: The RJ100ER has a range of 3,000km (1,865m). The RJ100LR is a long-range version giving 650km extra range. A 'hot-and-high' version with a GE CF34-3B1 engine option was introduced for 1996. Bombardier Canadair is now developing a larger 70-seat stablemate, the CRJ-700, powered by CF34-8 turbofans. The new version is due for delivery in 2003.

TWIN-ENGINED JET AIRLINERS

British Aerospace BAC One-Eleven

Twin-turbofan short-range airliner

Basic data for BAC One-Eleven Series 500

Powerplant: Two Rolls-Royce Spey 512-14DW turbofans of 12,550lb st (56kN)
Span: 93ft 6in (28.50m)
Length: 107ft 0in (32.61m)
Max Cruise: 541mph (871km/h)
Passengers: 119 plus two crew
First aircraft flown: 20 August 1963.
Production: 232 in UK (56 Series 200, nine Series 300, 69 Series 400, nine Series 475, 89 Series 500). Series 560 built by Romaero in Romania as the Rombac One-Eleven, the first aircraft being flown in September 1982 with nine aircraft produced.

Above:
BAC One-Eleven Srs 400s based in Oman have hush-kits fitted to their Rolls-Royce Spey engines.
PRM

Recent/current service: More than 120 are current with 30 airlines including AB Airlines, Aero Asia Int'l, British World AL, European Air Charter, JARO Int'l, Jersey European, Kabo Air, Maersk Air, Nationwide Air Charter, Okada Air, Oriental AL, Tarom and Zaire Express. Many One-Elevens are in corporate operation, particularly in North America.
Recognition: Engines mounted either side of the rear fuselage forward of the tail unit. Slightly swept wings set in the lower section of the circular narrow-body fuselage. T-tailplane mounted on top of

Above:
This BAC One-Eleven Srs 510ED is operated by
European Aircharter. *PRM*

the swept fin and rudder. Auxiliary power unit (APU) in the tail-cone.

Variants: Series 200, 300 and 400 have a short fuselage (93ft 6in/28.50m) and shorter span wings (88ft 8in/26.95m) and are broadly the same externally in appearance. The larger Series 500 has a 13ft 6in (4.14m) longer fuselage and a 5ft (1.55m) extended wingspan. The Series 475 has the short fuselage of the Series 400 and the bigger wings of the Series 500, together with a modified undercarriage with low-pressure tyres and larger wheels. Some aircraft have been retrofitted with a large forward freight door; others have powerplant hushkits. Development of a Stage 3 hushkit is being undertaken by US-based specialist Quiet Nacelle, in conjunction with European Aviation. Romaero plans to produce a Rolls-Royce Tay 650-powered One-Eleven-500, the 1-11-2500, or AirStar 2500.

Embraer ERJ-145 Amazon

Twin-turbofan regional airliner

Basic data for ERJ-145

Above:
The long slim fuselage of the ERJ-145 is evident in this photograph. DJM

Powerplant: Two Allison AE3007A turbofans of 7,033lb st (31.32kN)
Span: 65ft 9in (20.04m)
Length: 98ft 0in (29.87m)
Max Cruise: 479mph (770km/h)
Passengers: 50 plus two crew
First aircraft flown: 11 August 1995.
Production: Entered production 1996 with US risk-sharing partner C. & D. Interiors. 79 delivered by late 1998 with 215 ERJ-145s and 145 ERJ-135s on order (including 75 for AMR Eagle).
Recent/current service: Entered service in November 1996. Used by AMR Eagle, British Regional AL, Continental Express, Eastern Trade Wings, Flandre Air, Flight West AL, Luxair, National Jet Systems, Rio Sul, Skyways of Sweden, Trans States AL.
Recognition: The ERJ-145 is based on a stretched EMB-120 Brasilia fuselage, with pod-mounted turbofans on each side of the rear fuselage. It features a revised tail section and an all-new supercritical wing. Slim, circular fuselage with a large swept fin and rudder with dorsal projection. The swept tailplane is located on top of the fin. Pointed nose with sharply-raked large cockpit windscreens.
Variants: ERJ-145ER is the extended-range version. A shorter-fuselage 37-seat derivative, the ERJ-135, was flown on 4 July 1998. It has 90% commonality with the ERJ-145.

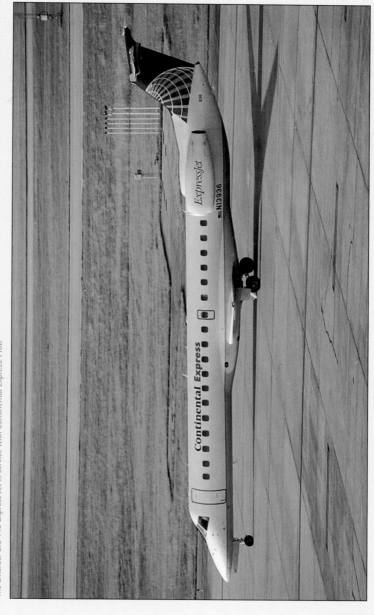

Below:
The Embraer ERJ-145 Express Jet in service with Continental Express. *PRM*

TWIN-ENGINED JET AIRLINERS

Fokker F28 Fellowship

Twin-turbofan short-range airliner

Basic data for Fokker F28-4000 Fellowship

Powerplant: Two Rolls-Royce RB183-2 Mk 555-15P turbofans of 9,900lb st (44kN)
Span: 82ft 3in (25.07m)
Length: 97ft 1in (29.62m)
Max Cruise: 515mph (830km/h)
Passengers: 85 plus two crew
First aircraft flown: 9 May 1967 (Mk 1000); 20 October 1976 (Mk 4000).
Production: 241 (production ceased in 1987) – some 170 still in operation in late 1998.
Recent/current service: The list of F28 operators includes Air Liberté, Air Nugini, Ansett Australia, Biman Bangladesh, Canadian Regional AL, Flight West AL, Garuda, Horizon AL, Iran Asseman AL, Libyan Arab AL, Merpati Nusantara, Myanmar AW, Pelita AS, SAS and US Airways.
Recognition: Engines mounted on the sides of the rear fuselage forward of the tail. Low-set wings in

Above:
A Fokker F28-100 Fellowship. *PRM*

the lower section of the circular, short fuselage. Swept fin with a rounded top and a dorsal fillet. Swept tailplane set at the top of the fin with a rounded section projecting above the tailplane. Sideways-opening airbrakes below the rudder.
Variants: Fokker Services has proposed a Rolls-Royce Tay 620 re-engining programme. F28 Mks 1000, 3000 and 5000 have shorter fuselages than the Mks 2000, 4000 and 6000; Mks 3000 to 6000 have extended wings, the Mks 5000 and 6000 with leading-edge slats.
Mk 1000 – span: 77ft 4in (23.57m), length: 89ft 11in (27.41m)
Mk 2000 – span: 77ft 4in (23.57m), length: 97ft 2in (29.62m)
Mk 3000 – span: 82ft 3in (25.07m), length: 89ft 11in (27.41m)
Mk 4000 – span: 82ft 3in (25.07m), length: 97ft 2in (29.62m)
Mk 5000 – span: 82ft 3in (25.07m), length: 89ft 11in (27.41m)
Mk 6000 – span: 82ft 3in (25.07m), length: 97ft 2in (29.62m)

Below:
Longer-fuselage Fokker F28-3000. *PRM*

Fokker 70/100

Twin-turbofan short/medium-range airliner

Basic data for Fokker 70 (standard)

Above:
KLM uk (previously Air UK) operates a fleet of Fokker 100s. *PRM*

Below:
A Fokker 100 of China Eastern, showing its slender wings and narrow fuselage. *PRM*

Powerplant: Two Rolls-Royce Tay 620 turbofans of 13,850lb st (61.6kN)
Span: 92ft 11½in (28.08m)
Length: 101ft 5in (30.91m)
Max Cruise: 531mph (854km/h)
Passengers: 80 plus two crew
First aircraft flown: 2 April 1993.
Production: By late 1998, 309 had been delivered. However, after Fokker went bankrupt, production had ceased in early 1997.
Recent/current service: Air France, Air Ivoire, Air Littoral, Alpi Eagles, American, Austrian AL, British Midland, Corse, Deutsche BA, Formosa AL, Gill Airways, Iran Air, KLM CityHopper, KLM uk, Korean Air, Malev, Merpati Nusantara, Mexicana, Midway AL, Pelita AS, Portugalia, Royal Brunei AL, Sempati Air, TAT European AL, Transwede, Tyrolean AW, US Airways and Vietnam AL.

Recognition: Engines mounted on the sides of the rear fuselage aft of the wing. Swept tailplane set at top of the fin which has a rounded top and dorsal fillet. Longer fuselage than the F28, circular in section; low-set swept wings.

Variants: The Fokker 100 is 15ft 3in (4.62m) longer and seats 107 passengers. It first flew on 30 November 1986. This superseded the F28-4000, from which it was derived. The Fokker 70ER is the Extended Range version. Fokker Executive Jet 70/Jet 100 are the corporate shuttle, business and VIP versions.

Twin-turbofan short/medium-range airliner

Above:
The larger size of the DC-9 range is the Series 41, shown here in SAS colours. PRM

Basic data for DC-9 Series 30

Powerplant: Two Pratt & Whitney JT8D-7 turbofans of 15,490lb st (62.3kN)
Span: 93ft 5in (28.47m)
Length: 119ft 4in (36.37m)
Max Cruise: 579mph (932km/h)
Passengers: 115 plus two crew
First aircraft flown: 25 February 1965 (Series 10); 1 August 1966 (Series 30); 28 November 1967 (Series 40).

Production: A total of 976 DC-9s (up to the Series 50) were built including 43 USAF/USN C-9s, of which 797 (including 500 Series 30)

were still in service by late 1998.

Recent/current service: With Adria, Aerocalifornia, Aeromexico, Air Canada, Airborne Express, AirTran, Alitalia, Aviaco, Binter Canarias, Cebu Pacific Air, Continental, Evergreen, Finnair, Hawaiian AL, Iberia, JAT, Meridiana, Midwest Express, Northwest, Spirit AL, Sun Air, TWA, US Airways, USA Jet AL and many others worldwide.

Recognition: Engines mounted on the sides of the rear fuselage forward of the fin. Low-set, swept wings which taper towards the wingtips. Narrow-body, circular fuselage with a rounded nose and pointed tail. Angular swept fin and rudder with a swept T-tailplane

Left:
A short-fuselage DC-9-30. PRM

mounted near the top. A small rounded fin extension above the tailplane with a bullet fairing to the rear.

Variants: The DC-9 has been extended in length and wingspan progressively from the Series 10 to the current production MD-80 series. There have also been DC-9C convertible and DC-9F freight variants, with large forward freight doors.

DC-9-10 – span: 89ft 5in (27.25m), length: 104ft 5in (31.83m)
DC-9-20 – span: 93ft 5in (28.47m), length: 104ft 5in (31.83m)
DC-9-30 – span: 93ft 5in (28.47m), length: 119ft 4in (36.37m)
DC-9-40 – span: 93ft 5in (28.47m), length: 125ft 8in (38.30m)
DC-9-50 – span: 93ft 5in (28.47m), length: 133ft 7in (40.72m)

The different models also have changes in powerplants, all-up-weights, internal improvements and in other areas. ABS Partnership offers an FAA-approved Stage 3 hushkit for the type and Raisbeck Commercial Group is developing an aerodynamic Stage 3 solution similar to that it offers for the Boeing 727.

SATIC A300-600ST Beluga

Left:
The whale-like appearance of the SATIC Beluga. *PRM*

Below:
The massive fuselage is well illustrated in this view of the SATIC Beluga. *PRM*

Twin-turbofan very large transport aircraft

Basic data for SATIC A300-608ST

Powerplant: Two General Electric CF6-80C2A8 turbofans of 57,600lb st (256kN)
Span: 147ft 2in (44.84m)
Length: 184ft 3in (56.15m)
Max Cruise: 484.15mph (778.8km/h)
Payload: 47 tonnes/103,616lb (47,098kg)
First aircraft flown: 13 September 1994.
Production: The Special Aircraft Transport International Company A300-600 Super Transporter – also commonly known as the Beluga – is built by the Aérospatiale/Daimler-Benz Aerospace 50:50 consortium, SATIC. Four have been delivered by

late 1998, a fifth was ordered by Airbus in 1998, and a sixth in early 1999, for delivery in 2001/2002, which will enable one aircraft to be dedicated to third-party contract work.
Recent/current service: The first four are operated by Airbus Inter Transport to carry large aircraft sub-assemblies, and have been used for other duties such as the carrying of helicopters.
Recognition: Based on new-build A300-600R airframes with an upward-opening nose section, 7.4m diameter fuselage, and a lowered flightdeck based on that of the A320. An enlarged fin and horizontal tail end-plates to improve directional stability. Has 400cu m greater volume than that of the Aerospacelines Super Guppy which it has replaced and 22.5 tonnes greater payload capacity.
Variants: None as yet, but SATIC is considering the Beluga concept on other airframes, such as the A340, to provide even larger outsized-cargo capability.

AIRBUS INDUSTRIE

Left:
The Tupolev Tu-134A is widely used by airlines in the former Russian states. *PRM*

Below:
Balkan Bulgarian operates the twin-engined Tu-134A. *DJM*

Twin-turbofan medium-range airliner

Basic data for Tupolev Tu-134A

Powerplant: Two Soloviev D-30-II turbofans of 14,990lb st (66.75kN)
Span: 95ft 2in (29.01m)
Length: 121ft 7in (37.06m)
Max Cruise: 550mph (885km/h)
Passengers: 80 plus three crew
First aircraft flown: July 1963.
Production: 852 built, with 365 in airline service as of late 1998. Production ended 1985.
Recent/current service: Used by Aeroflot Russian Int'l AL, Air Moldova, Air Ukraine, Arkhangelsk AL, Belavia, Donavia, Kaliningrad, Kazakhstan AW, Komiavia, Syrianair, Tyumen AL and Vietnam AL amongst others.
Recognition: Engines mounted high on the sides of the rear fuselage below the dorsal fin. Well-swept wings mounted on the bottom of the slim, circular fuselage, with large undercarriage fairings extending from the trailing-edges of the wings. A broad, slightly swept fin and rudder with the very swept tailplane mounted on top. Bullet fairings project forward and rear of the fin/tailplane junction. Some early versions had a glazed nose and chin radome.
Variants: The original Tu-134 had a 6ft 11in (2.11m) shorter fuselage than the major production version, the Tu-134A. The Tu-134B had a revised flightdeck with no navigator, and also introduced modified spoilers. Russian and Ukrainian engine manufacturers are touting re-engineering programmes for the large number of Tu-134s which remain in service across Russia and other former USSR states.

Twin-turbofan medium-range airliner

Basic data for Tupolev Tu-204-100

Powerplant: Two Aviadvigatel PS-90A turbofans of 35,275lb st (157.13kN) or Rolls-Royce RB211-535E4Bs of 43,043lb st (191.3kN)
Span: 137ft 9in (42.0m)
Length: 157ft 6in (48.00m)
Max Cruise: 528mph (850km/h)
Passengers: 240 plus two crew
First aircraft flown: 2 January 1989.
Production: 40 aircraft are on order from Russian carriers with 16 delivered.
Recent/current service: Ten in service during late 1998 with Aeroflot Russian Int'l AL, Air Cairo, Perm AL, Tupolev-Aerotrans and Vnukovo.
Recognition: Large fan engines with round nacelles mounted under and forward of the swept wings (that have winglets). Circular, slim fuselage with low-set wings. Tall,

Above:
The Tu-204 entered service with Vnukovo Airlines in 1994. *PRM*

Below:
The Tu-204 features large fan engines mounted forward of the slender pointed wings that feature winglets. *PRM*

angular, swept fin and rudder. Swept tailplane set on the rear fuselage at the base of the rudder.
Variants: The Rolls-Royce-powered version (two 193kN/43,338lb st RB211-535E4s) is now designated as the Tu-204-120 and marketed by Sirocco Aerospace International. The Tu-204-200 is now known as the Tu-214.

69

Four-turboprop STOL short-range airliner

Basic data for DHC Dash 7-100

Powerplant: Four Pratt & Whitney PT6A-50 turboprops of 1,150shp (857kW)
Span: 93ft 0in (28.35m)
Length: 80ft 8in (24.59m)
Max Cruise: 265mph (426km/h)
Passengers: 50 plus two crew
First aircraft flown: 27 March 1975.
Production: 113 built for 35 customers in 22 countries. Production ceased in 1988.
Recent/current service: 78 in use with Arkia, Brymon Offshore Air Charter, Far Airlines, Greenlandair, LTA, Paradise Island AW, Piedmont AL, Pelita AS, Tyrolean AW, Voyageur AW, Wideroe, Yemenia and others.
Recognition: Four turboprops, each with four-blade propellers, mounted

Above:
DHC7-110 Dash 7 operated by Brymon Offshore Airways/British Airways. *PRM*

Below:
A Dash 7 using its STOL capabilities for landing. *PRM*

below the straight wing, which has distinctive trailing flaps. The circular fuselage is set below the wing, tapering upwards towards the tail. Very large swept fin and rudder with a dorsal extension; a straight tailplane is mounted on top of the fin.
Variants: Initial production aircraft were either Series 100 passenger or Series 101 cargo variants. These were superseded by the Series 150 and 151, which offered higher operating weights and fuel capacity.

Above:
A DC-6A operated by cargo carrier Atlantic Air Transport. *PRM*

Four-piston-engined medium-range transport

Basic data for Douglas DC-4

Powerplant: Four Pratt & Whitney R-2000-25D-13G piston engines of 1,450hp (1,081kW)
Span: 117ft 6in (35.81m)
Length: 93ft 5in (28.47m)
Max Cruise: 204mph (328km/h)
Passengers: 44 plus three crew
First aircraft flown: 21 June 1938 (DC-4E); 14 February 1942 (C-54).
Production: Over 2,350 of the DC-4, -6, -7 series built including military versions.
Recent/current service: Approximately 200 (76 DC-4s, 104 DC-6s and 20 DC-7s) remain in service in late 1998 with small airlines mainly in North and South America including Aero Union, American Air Freight, ARDCO, Central AS, Conifair, Conair

Aviation, Everts Air Fuel, Millardair, Northern AC and Trans-Air Link. Also with Atlantic AL for cargo and pollution control taskings in the UK.
Recognition: Four piston engines mounted on the tapered and dihedralled wings, which are set in the lower section of the circular fuselage. Rear, top fuselage tapers downwards; the straight fin and rudder has a curved top edge. The low-set tailplane is located on either side of the tail cone below the fin and rudder. Oval cabin windows and a large freight door on the port side of the converted ex-military aircraft.
Variants: The Canadair C-54M was a variant built in Canada and powered by Rolls-Royce Merlin engines – none remains in airline service. The Carvair was a DC-4 modified as a car-ferry/freighter, with a raised cockpit and distinctive bulbous, opening

71

nose and a modified fin and rudder. The DC-6 was a pressurised, longer development of the DC-4, with more powerful engines and other internal changes. The DC-7 was further increased in performance and internal refinement.

DC-6 – span: 117ft 6in (35.81m), length: 100ft 7in (30.66m), 52 passengers

DC-6A – span: 117ft 6in (35.81m), length: 105ft 7in (32.18m), and modified, more angular fin and rudder, with fore and aft freight doors

DC-6B – span: 117ft 6in (35.81m), length: 106ft 8in (32.51m), with nose weather radar. Fitted as passenger transport

DC-6C – modified DC-6A to passenger configuration

DC-7 – span: 117ft 6in (35.81m), length: 108ft 11in (33.20m), more

Above:
South African Airways Historic Flight continues to operate the Douglas DC-4. PRM

powerful engines, and modified forward fuselage

DC-7B – span: 117ft 6in (35.81m), length: 108ft 11in (33.20m)

DC-7C – span: 127ft 6in (38.86m), length: 112ft 3in (34.21m), long-range development with increased span and fuselage length, 107 passengers

DC-7F – span: 127ft 6in (38.86m), length: 112ft 3in (34.21m), freighter conversion with port-side front cargo door and an extra large rear fuselage loading door

Four-turboprop long-range airliner

Basic data for Ilyushin Il-18E

Above:
The turboprop Il-18 has now been replaced by most of the major East European carriers. *PRM*

Below:
A number of Russian-built Ilyushin Il-18s continue to be operated by charter and cargo companies. *Peter Busby*

Powerplant: Four Ivchenko AI-20M turboprops of 4,250shp (3,170kW)
Span: 122ft 8½in (37.40m)
Length: 117ft 9in (35.89m)
Max Cruise: 419mph (674km/h)
Passengers: 110 plus five crew
First aircraft flown: 4 July 1957.
Production: Over 700 built up to 1969, mainly for Aeroflot, with at least 474 remaining in service in late 1998. Production terminated in 1970.
Recent/current service: With Aero Caribbean, Air Koryo, Elf Air and others.
Recognition: Four turboprops mounted above the straight wing which is set in the lower section of the long, circular fuselage. Tall, slender fin and rudder with a small dorsal extension. Straight tailplane set on either side of the fuselage below the rudder.
Variants: Little external difference between the Il-18D, Il-18E, Il-18L and Il-18V production aircraft, which have revised powerplants and internal layouts. More than 71 are in service as freighters.

Lockheed Electra

Four-turboprop medium-range transport

Basic data for L-188AF Electra

Powerplant: Four Allison 501-D13 turboprops of 3,750shp (2,796kW)
Span: 99ft 0in (30.18m)
Length: 104ft 6in (31.85m)
Max Cruise: 405mph (652km/h)
Passengers: Three crew
First aircraft flown: 6 December 1957.
Production: 170 built with 61 in freight service during late 1998.
Recent/current service: Used by Atlantic AL, Blue AL, Channel Express, Daylight Air, Fred Olsen, Interlink of Congo, Lynden Air Cargo, Reeve Aleutian, Transafrik, Zantop Int'l AL and others.

Above:
The four-turboprop Lockheed Electra is used exclusively for freight operations. *PRM*

Right:
The Lockheed Electra has a distinctive dihedral tailplane set at the extreme rear of the fuselage. *Peter Busby*

Recognition: Four turboprops widely spaced on the broad-chord, short-span, square-tipped wings. Circular fuselage mounted above the wing. Shaped fin and rudder with a dorsal extension. Tailplane set on top of the rear fuselage below the fin and rudder.
Variants: No external differences between the L-188AF and L-188CF. All Electras remaining in service have been converted for freight operations with one or more large cargo loading doors on the port side of the fuselage.

Lockheed L-100 Hercules

Four-turboprop long-range transport

Basic data for L-100-30 Hercules

Powerplant: Four Allison 501-D22A turboprops of 4,508shp (3,399kW)
Span: 132ft 7in (40.41m)
Length: 112ft 9in (34.37m)
Max Cruise: 363mph (584km/h)
Passengers: 97 plus three crew; maximum payload 51,402lb (23,315kg)
First aircraft flown: 23 August 1954 (military YC-130); 21 April 1964 (L-382 airline variant).
Production: Only 115 civilian aircraft built from over 2,200 C-130s by late 1998.
Recent/current service: Operators are Aer Lingus, Air Algérie, Air China, Air Foyle, Angola Air Charter, HeavyLift Cargo AL, Libyan Arab AL, Pelita, Safair and Transafrik Int'l. The main civilian operator of L-100s, Southern Air Transport, went into receivership and ceased operations in August 1998.
Recognition: Four turboprops located under high-set straight

Above:
One of a number of Lockheed L-100-30 Hercules in use by HeavyLift. Peter Busby

wing. A circular fuselage with a distinctive nose radome, undercarriage fairings and upswept tail for rear cargo loading. Tall, shaped fin and rudder with a small dorsal extension forward of the fin. Tailplane at the extremity of the fuselage at the base of the fin and rudder. Few cabin windows.
Variants: The original L-382 was similar to the C-130E Hercules. Subsequent civil variants have had longer fuselages; L-100-20 was 8ft 4in (2.54m) longer and the L-100-30 was 20ft (6.10m) longer. Over 86 variants of the civil and military Hercules have been produced and are in service in 60 countries. An L-100-30 belonging to Merpati Nusantara has been certified by the FAA as a 97-seat airliner. The L-100J is the proposed commercial version of the new-generation C-130J Hercules, which first flew December 1995, initially as a freighter. It has Allison AE2100D3 turboprops and Dowty R391 six-bladed propellers.

Below:
An L-100 that was operated by Southern Air Transport. *PRM*

Twin-turboprop short-range transport

Basic data for An-26

Powerplant: Two Ivchenko AI-24VT turboprops of 2,820shp (2,103kW)
Span: 95ft 9½in (29.20m)
Length: 78ft 1in (23.8m)
Max Cruise: 270mph (435km/h)
Passengers: 38-40 plus three crew
First aircraft flown: 20 December 1959 (An-24); 21 May 1969 (An-26); 9 July 1977 (An-32).
Production: Over 2,100 An-24/26s built of which some 1,453 are in airline service, together with a further 212 An-30/32s.
Recent/current service: With Aeroflot Russian Int'l AL and its successor airlines, Aero Caribbean, Aero Gaviota, Air Guinee, Air Kazakhstan, Air Ukraine, Air Urga, Atran, Balkan, Cubana, Iraqi AW, Lithuanian AL, Tarom, Uzbekistan AW and many more in Eastern Europe and Asia.
Recognition: Large twin turboprops mounted below and extending in front of and behind the wings, which

Above:
The Polish airline LOT Cargo operates this An-26.
PRM

Below:
The An-32 is identified by the raised engine line above the wing. PRM

taper sharply outboard of the engines. The circular-section fuselage is set under the wings. A tall fin and rudder with a forward dorsal extension. The tailplane is mounted below the rudder on the fuselage. There is a ventral fin below the tail.
Variants: The An-24T is an all-cargo version; the An-26 has a rear-loading ramp; the An-30 is a developed aerial survey version with a new front fuselage; the An-32 is a more powerful version of the An-26, with Progress/Ivchenko AI-20D Series 5 turboprops of 5,112shp (3,812kW) and a raised engine line well above the top of the fuselage, seating 50 passengers. The An-24 is manufactured in China as the Xian Y-7H.

Left:
The ATR-42 has a high-set wing, distinctive shaped fin and rudder and tailplane set near to the top of the fin. *DJM*

Below:
An ATR-42 operated by the Dutch airline Air Exel. *PRM*

Twin-turboprop regional airliner

Basic data for ATR 42-300

Powerplant: Two Pratt & Whitney Canada PW120-2 turboprops of 2,000shp (1,491kW)
Span: 80ft 7in (24.57m)
Length: 74ft 4⅓in (22.67m)
Max Cruise: 307mph (495km/h) at 20,000ft
Passengers: Maximum seating for 50 plus two crew
First aircraft flown: 16 August 1984; July 1995 (ATR 42-400).
Production: 334 produced for 67 airlines by late 1998 with a further 15 on order.
Recent/current service: Operated by Aeromar, Air Botswana, Air Caledonie, Air Littoral, Air Tahiti, Alitalia Express, AMR Eagle, Brit Air, British Airways/CityFlyer Express, Canadian Regional AL, Cimber Air, Comair, Continental Express, Croatia, CSA, Eurowings, Flagship AL, Gill AW, Inter-Canadian, Italair, Olympic Aviation, Oman Air, Tarom, TAT European AL, Titan AW, Trans States AL and other commuter airlines.
Recognition: High-set straight wing with slim engines projecting forward and below the wing close inboard. Circular-section fuselage with large undercarriage fairings under the centre section. Distinctive, large, slightly swept fin and rudder with two angle changes on the forward edge. Straight tailplane set near to the top of the fin.
Variants: Two basic versions, the ATR 42-200 and -300, the latter with increased payload/range. ATR 42F is a version with larger port-side door; ATR 42R has a rear fuselage loading ramp. ATR 42-320 has more powerful P&W 121 engines for hot-and-high performance. The ATR 42-400 has 1,600kW P&WC turboprops, fitted with six-bladed propellers and the Czech carrier CSA became the first airline to take delivery in March 1996. ATR 42-500 has improved performance from P&W Canada 127Es driving six-blade propellers. First flown 16 September 1994 and deliveries commenced mid-1995 to Continental Express.

Avions de Transport Regional ATR 72

Twin-turboprop regional airliner

Basic data for ATR 72-210

Above:
This ATR-72 of American Eagle shows its considerable fuselage 'stretch' over the ATR-42.
PRM

Powerplant: Two Pratt & Whitney Canada PW127 turboprops of 2,475shp (2,050kW)
Span: 88ft 9in (27.05m)
Length: 89ft 5in (27.16m)
Max Cruise: 327mph (526km/h)
Passengers: Up to 74 plus 2 crew
First aircraft flown: 27 October 1988.
Production: 211 delivered by late 1998 with a further 10 on order.
Recent/current service: With Air Greece, Air Tahiti, AMR Eagle, Arkia Israeli AL, Binter Canarias, Brit Air, China Xinjiang AL, CityFlyer Express, Corse Mediterranée, CSA, EuroLOT, Euroscot Express, Eurowings, Finnair, Gill AW, Iran Asseman AL, KLM uk, Mount Cook AL, Olympic, Thai, Transasia AW, Vietnam AL and a number of US commuter airlines.

Recognition: Similar to but longer than the ATR 42. High-set wing with slim engines projecting forward and below the wing. Circular-section fuselage with large undercarriage fairings under the centre section. Large, slightly swept fin and rudder with two angle changes on the forward edge. Tailplane set near to the top of the fin.
Variants: The ATR 72 is a stretched (by 15ft/4.9m) development of the ATR 42. It is the first airliner with a carbon-fibre wingbox. An ATR 72 with a further stretch, to seat 82 passengers, is scheduled to fly in 1996. A high-speed ATR 72-500 is due for first deliveries in 1999 with six-bladed propellers. The ATR 82 is a proposed larger-capacity and higher-performance development of the ATR regional airliners.

Bombardier (De Havilland) Dash 8

Left:
A Brymon Airways Dash 8 Series 300 flies in the colours of its owner British Airways. *PRM*

Below:
The high-wing de Havilland Canada Dash 8-300 has a STOL performance. *PRM*

Twin-turboprop regional airliner

Basic data for Dash 8 Series 300B

Powerplant: Two Pratt & Whitney Canada PW123B turboprops of 2,500shp (1,865kW)
Span: 90ft 9in (27.43m)
Length: 84ft 3in (25.68m)
Max Cruise: 327mph (527km/h)
Passengers: 56 with two crew
First aircraft flown: 20 June 1983 (DHC-8-100); 15 May 1987 (DHC-8-300).
Production: By the end of 1998, 498 Dash 8s had been delivered with a further 73 on order.
Recent/current service: With 58 airlines including Air BC, Ansett New Zealand, Augsburg AW, Bahamasair, British Airways/Brymon, Canadian Regional AL, Eastern Australia AL, Great China AL, Horizon Air, SA Express, Sabena, Sunstate AL, Tyrolean AW, Wideroes, Zhejang AL and many US commuter airlines.

Recognition: Narrow-profile turboprops set underneath high-set, narrow-chord, unswept wings. Circular fuselage section which sweeps up to a broad, slightly swept, rectangular fin and rudder. Dorsal extension reaches forward to the trailing-edge of the wing. Straight tailplane set on top of the fin. Streamlined nose with a continuous line down from the cockpit.

Variants: The Series 200 is a higher-powered version of the Series 100 with P&WC PW123 engines. Series 300 has a longer (11ft 6in) fuselage to accommodate up to 56 passengers, and Pratt & Whitney PW123 turboprops. The Dash 8M is a military version of the Series 100. A combi version has a large inward-opening door for cargo loading. The Series 400, seating 70-78 passengers was launched in June 1995. Powered by two 3,598kW PW150 turboprops, and capable of cruising at 647km/h, Dash 8Q-400 first flew on 31 January 1998. Bombardier has now entitled the Dash 8 family as the Q Series (Q for Quiet), consisting of the 37-seat Q-200, 50-seat Q-300 and the new Q-400.

TWIN-ENGINED PROPELLER AIRLINERS

British Aerospace HS748

Twin-turboprop short-range transport

Above:
An HS748 in the colours of Emerald Airways. PRM

Basic data for HS748 Series 2B

Powerplant: Two Rolls-Royce Dart 552 turboprops of 2,280shp (1,700kW)
Span: 102ft 6in (31.23m)
Length: 67ft 0in (20.42m)
Max Cruise: 277mph (447km/h)
Passengers: 52 plus two crew
First aircraft flown: 24 June 1960; 30 August 1961 (Series 1); 6 November 1961 (Series 2); 5 September 1967 (Series 2B).
Production: 382 built, including 18 Series 1. Production ceased 1988.
Recent/current service: 122 in airline service with 48 airlines worldwide including Aero Service, Air Creebec, Air Inuit, Air Madagascar, Air Manitoba, Air Senegal, Airfast Indonesia, Bahamasair, Bouraq Indonesia, Emerald AW, First Air, Ibis Air Transport, ITAB, Merpati and West Air Sweden.

Recognition: Twin turboprops mounted above and forward of the low-set wing, with the undercarriage fairing beneath. Wings have dihedral and taper towards the tips. A broad, unswept fin and rudder with a dorsal fillet. Low-set tailplane either side of the lower rear fuselage. Some versions have a large, port-side freight loading door.

Variants: The Series 1, 2 and 2A are all externally similar. The Series 2B has a 4ft (1.22m) extension to the wingspan and an optional freight door. The final variant was the Super 748, based on the 2B, with a new flightdeck, hush-kit engines and water-methanol injection. Some 90 748s were produced under licence by Hindustan Aeronautics (HAL) in India.

Twin-turboprop regional airliner

Basic data for Jetstream 61

Powerplant: Two Pratt & Whitney Canada PW127D turboprops of 2,750shp (2,051kW)
Span: 100ft 6in (30.63m)
Length: 85ft 4in (26.01m)
Max Cruise: 311mph (500km/h)
Passengers: Maximum of 72 plus two crew
First aircraft flown: 6 August 1986 (ATP); 10 May 1994 (Jetstream 61).
Production: 60 ATPs produced

Above:
The BAe ATP/Jetstream 61 succeeded the HS748 in production, from which it was developed. *DJM*

Below:
An ATP/Jetstream 61 in the colours of Manx Airlines. *DJM*

when production ceased in 1994. With completion of ATP deliveries production switched to the improved Jetstream 61 but this has now ended.

Recent/current service: 52 in use as of late 1998, operators including Air Europa Express, Bangladesh Biman, British Airways (to phase its ATPs out in early 1999), British Regional AW, British World AL, Canarias Regional Air, Jersey European, Manx AL, Merpati Nusantara AL, SATA and United Feeder Service.

Recognition: Resembles a stretched HS748 with twin turboprops mounted above and forward of the low-set wings. The fuselage, circular in section, is stretched forward and aft of the wings. Redesigned swept fin and rudder and modified, more pointed nose. The current Jetstream 61 has uprated engines, increased maximum take-off weight and cabin improvements.

Variants: The last five ATPs off the line were configured so that they can be converted for cargo operations.

British Aerospace Jetstream Super 31

Twin-turboprop commuter airliner

Basic data for Jetstream Super 31

Above:
This Jetstream 31 operated by Air Kilroe is fitted with an under-fuselage luggage pack. *PRM*

Below:
The Jetstream 31 was developed from the Astazou-powered Handley Page Jetstream. *PRM*

Powerplant: Two Garrett TPE331-12UAR turboprops of 1,020shp (761kW)
Span: 52ft 0in (15.85m)
Length: 47ft 1½in (14.36m)
Max Cruise: 303mph (488km/h)
Passengers: 19 plus one/two crew
First aircraft flown: 18 March 1980; 13 April 1988 (Jetstream Super 31); the original Handley Page Jetstream was flown on 18 August 1967.
Production: 390 Jetstream 31/Super 31s delivered when production ceased in 1993. The USA's regional airline industry was the biggest market.
Recent/current service: With Air BC, Air Kilroe, CCAir, Chautauqua AL, Chicago Express, Eastern Australia, European Executive Express, Express Airlines, Flying Enterprise, Maersk Air, NPA/Westair, Origin Pacific AW, Regional AL,

Skywest, Trans States AL/Trans World Express and many others.
Recognition: Twin turboprops mounted above and forward of the low-set wings. Circular fuselage with a long, pointed nose forward of the cockpit. Swept, tall fin and rudder with a triangular ventral extension. Circular cabin windows and a passenger door aft of the port wing.
Variants: The original Jetstream had Turbomeca Astazou XIV turboprops which are more slender and extend further forward of the wing, with a distinctive long spinner. The Super 31 has uprated engines (Garrett TPE331-12 turboprops), an improved cabin and increased maximum take-off weight.

Twin-turboprop commuter airliner

Basic data for Jetstream 41

Powerplant: Two Garrett TPE331-14HR/GR turboprops of 1,650shp (1,230kW)
Span: 60ft 5in (18.42m)
Length: 63ft 2in (19.25m)
Max Cruise: 339mph (547km/h)
Passengers: 29 plus one/two crew
First aircraft flown: 25 September 1991.
Production: 100 delivered by the end of 1998 when production ceased.
Recent/current service: Atlantic Coast AL/United Express, British Midland, British Regional AL, Maersk Air, Manx AL/BA Express, SA AirLink

Above:
The Jetstream 41 is a 16ft-stretched version with engines giving 50% more power than the -31. *PRM*

Below:
With a longer fuselage, modified wing and tail, the Jetstream 41 is quite distinct in appearance from the smaller 31. *PRM*

and Trans States AL/Trans World Express.
Recognition: Twin turboprops mounted above and forward of the low-set wings. Circular fuselage with a long nose. Slim wings with straight leading-edges set at the bottom of the fuselage with a bulged fairing extending forward and aft of the wing. Swept fin and rudder, with mid-set tailplane and long dorsal extension. Circular cabin windows and a passenger door forward of the port wing and baggage loading access to the rear.
Variants: None produced, although 50- and 70-seat versions with new wings and larger engines were projected.

Britten-Norman Islander

Left:
The Islander with its fixed undercarriage, high wing and angular fuselage continues to be sold to air taxi and commuter operators worldwide. *PRM*

Below:
The rugged Islander is well suited to the operations of the Canadian company Lab Air. *APM*

Twin-piston/turboprop light transport

Basic data for BN-2T Turbine Islander

Powerplant: Two Allison 250-B17C turboprops of 400shp (298kW)
Span: 49ft 0in (14.94m) (53ft [16.15m] with extended wingtip tanks)
Length: 35ft 7¾in (10.86m)
Max Cruise: 196mph (315km/h)
Passengers: Nine plus one crew
First aircraft flown: 13 June 1965 (BN-2 Continental IO-360); 6 April 1977 (Turbo Islander Lycoming LTP101); 2 August 1980 (BN-2T Allison 250).
Production: Over 1,200 delivered by mid-1996. A production line is located in Romania (IAV Bucuresti). Approx 20 BN-2s per year are made, ownership of Britten-Norman having transferred in July 1998 from Switzerland's Oerlikon Bührle to Litchfield Continental.
Recent/current service: 385 operators worldwide, flying 1,214 examples in total as of late 1998, mainly commuter and air taxi airlines.

Recognition: Engines mounted below and forward of the straight, high-set 'plank' wing. Fixed tricycle undercarriage with the main wheels on an extended, faired leg at the rear of the engines and the nose-wheel situated well forward below the nose cone. Slab-sided rectangular fuselage with a level top surface and gently raked lower surface aft of the wing, two port-side cabin entry doors and large rectangular cabin windows. The tall, angular fin and rudder has a small dorsal fillet; the straight tailplane is mounted on top of the fuselage, below the rudder. The extended wingtips on some aircraft have a distinctive conical camber.
Variants: The BN-2, BN-2A and BN-2B are all broadly similar piston-engined versions. The latter two variants could have optional extras which include a lengthened nose forward of the cockpit and/or 4ft (1.22m) extended wingtips. The BN-2T has smaller Allison 250 turboprops in place of the Lycoming series piston engines.

Twin-turboprop commuter airliner and light transport

Above:
The high-wing CASA C-212 Aviocar has a box-like fuselage. *DJM*

Basic data for C-212-300 Aviocar

Powerplant: Two AlliedSignal Garrett TPE331-10R-513C turboprops of 900shp (671kW)
Span: 66ft 6½in (20.28m)
Length: 52ft 11½in (16.15m)
Max Cruise: 220mph (354km/h)
Passengers: 23-26 plus one/two crew
First aircraft flown: 26 March 1971 (Series 200); 1984 (Series 300)
Production: Over 500 sold in 35 countries for civil and military use, including about a quarter built under licence by Nurtanio in Indonesia.
Recent/current service: Some 88 flown by numerous commuter airlines in the US and non-scheduled airlines in Europe.

Recognition: Twin turboprops mounted forward of the high, straight wing, with winglets. A rectangular fuselage with a short, pointed nose and upswept rear section. An angular fin and rudder with a large dorsal extension. Undercarriage fairings on the lower fuselage below the wing. Tailplane positioned below the fin and rudder on an extension of the fuselage.

Variants: The initial production Series 100 had lower power turbo-props; Series 200 is externally similar. The latest Series 300 is larger, with a modified nose and a reshaped rear fuselage in place of the rear loading ramp, and features winglets. A PT6A-powered C-212P is available. The C-212-400 version is powered by 835kW TPE331-2RJ engines, and was flown in April 1997.

CASA-IPTN CN-235

Left:
Developed jointly in Spain and Indonesia as an enlarged C-212, the CN-235 has a much more streamlined appearance. *APM*

Below:
Binter Canarias is one of the airlines to operate the CN-235. *DJM*

Twin-turboprop regional airliner and light cargo transport

Basic data for CN-235-100

Powerplant: Two General Electric CT7-9C turboprops of 1,750shp (1,305kW)
Span: 84ft 8in (25.81m)
Length: 70ft 2½in (21.4m)
Max Cruise: 286mph (446km/h) at 15,000ft
Passengers: 45 plus two crew
First aircraft flown: 11 November 1983 (Spain), 31 December 1983 (Indonesia).
Production: Jointly manufactured by CASA (Spain) and IPTN (of Bandung, Indonesia). 25 delivered by late 1998, the last civil delivery having been made during 1993, plus 130 military versions (CN-235M).
Recent/current service: Austral Express,

Binter Canarias, Binter Mediterraneo and Merpati Nusantara.
Recognition: Twin turboprops set forward and under the high-mounted, tapered wings with extended tips. Large undercarriage fairings set under the circular fuselage centre section; rear fuselage swept up with rear loading ramp. Tall, swept fin and rudder with a long dorsal fairing. Straight tailplane set below the fin and rudder.
Variants: The CN-235-20, featuring a higher operating weight, refined rudder and tail was introduced in March 1992. A combi version to carry 19 passengers plus freight is also available (CN-235QC). CN-235MPA is the maritime patrol version. A larger CASA C-295, based on the CN-235, made its first flight on 28 November 1997.

Twin-piston-engined short-range airliner

Basic data for Convair CV-440

Powerplant: Two Pratt & Whitney R-2800-CB17 piston engines of 2,500hp (1,864kW)
Span: 105ft 4in (32.11m)
Length: 81ft 6in (24.84m)
Max Cruise: 300mph (483km/h)
Passengers: 56 plus two/three crew
First aircraft flown: 8 July 1946 (CV-110); 16 March 1947 (CV-240).
Production: A total of 968 of all models (up to CV-440) for civil and military use.
Recent/current service: Over 70 remain in service, mainly in the USA, with Cool Air, Frigorifico Reyes, Trans

Above:
A piston-engined Convair 440 operated for light freight services in California. PRM

Below:
The piston-engined Convair 440 serves with a handful of airlines, mainly as light freighters. PRM

Florida, Air Resorts Airlines, Kitty Hawk and others.
Recognition: Twin piston engines projecting forward of the tapered, low-set wing which has dihedral towards the tips. A circular fuselage with a shaped fin and rudder having a distinctive curved leading edge. The tailplane is set on the sides of the rear fuselage below the fin and rudder.
Variants: CV-240 – original short-fuselage (74ft 8in/22.76m) production version; CV-340 – has a 4ft 6in (1.37m) longer fuselage and broader chord wings; CV-440 – same fuselage as the 340 with modified engine cowlings and internal improvements. Nose lengthened by 2ft 4in (0.71m) when weather radar incorporated.

Convair 540, 580, 600 and 640

Twin-turboprop short-range airliner

Basic data for Convair 580

Above:
A Convair 580 operated by DHL in Europe for parcel freight. Peter Busby

Below:
Allison turboprops give a slimmer profile to this New Zealand-registered Convair 640.
Brian Strickland

Powerplant: Two Allison 501-D31H turboprops of 3,750shp (2,796kW)
Span: 105ft 4in (32.11m)
Length: 81ft 6in (24.84m)
Max Cruise: 342mph (550km/h)
Passengers: 56 plus two/three crew
First aircraft flown: 19 January 1960 (Convair 580).
Production: Total of 243 converted to turboprop standard from earlier models. 115 still in service in late 1998.
Recent/current service: Several North American provincial airlines including Air Chathams, Air Freight NZ, Air Venezuela, Canair Cargo, DHL Int'l, ERA Aviation, Kelowna, Kitty Hawk Air Transport and Zantop Int'l. European Air Transport and Swiftair are the only European operators with 580s.

Recognition: As Convair CV-240/440 with twin turboprops replacing the earlier piston engines. This gives a slimmer engine profile. The 580, 600 and 640 series all have the longer nose incorporating a weather radar. It has a larger fin for better single-engined stability.
Variants: Convair 580 has Allison 501-D31H turboprops; Convair 600 is a R-R Dart 10 Mk 524-engined conversion of the CV-240, and the Convair 640 is a similarly-engined conversion of the CV-340/440. The Convair 5800, a stretched version developed in British Columbia, first flew on 11 February 1992 and entered service in January 1994.

Twin-turboprop commuter transport

Basic data for DHC-6 Twin Otter Series 300

Above:
The STOL DHC Twin Otter is operated on routes into airports with short runways or difficult approaches. PRM

Powerplant: Two Pratt & Whitney PT6A-27 turboprops of 620shp (462kW)
Span: 65ft 0in (19.81m)
Length: 51ft 9in (15.77m)
Max Cruise: 209mph (336km/h)
Passengers: 20 plus two crew
First aircraft flown: 20 May 1965.
Production: 844 had been produced, including military models, when production ceased December 1988.
Recent/current service: Many feeder and commuter airlines worldwide use DHC-6s, 550 remaining in service at the end of 1998.
Recognition: Twin turboprops situated below and forward of the high-set 'plank' wing. A fixed tricycle undercarriage with the main wheels attached to the lower fuselage below the wing. Bracing struts extend from the undercarriage fairings to the engines. A flat-sided cabin with small, square windows set high up. Tapered rear fuselage and a long nose forward of the cockpit. The fin and rudder is tall, slightly tapered and square cut at the top, with the tailplane mounted near to the base.
Variants: Series 100 had a short nose. Series 200 features an extended nose, and the Series 300 has the longer nose and uprated engines. An upgrade programme is underway by Field Aviation of Canada, which includes the fitting of four-blade propellers.

Douglas DC-3 Dakota

Twin-piston-engined short-range transport

Above:
A landing view of South Coast Airways' DC-3. PRM

Basic data for Douglas DC-3

Powerplant: Two Pratt & Whitney R-1830-92 Twin Wasp piston engines of 1,200hp (894kW)
Span: 95ft 0in (28.96m)
Length: 64ft 6in (19.66m)
Max Cruise: 194mph (312km/h)
Passengers: 32 plus two crew
First aircraft flown: 17 December 1935.
Production: 10,962 built of which only 458 were originally for civilian use. Some 450 remain in commercial use today.
Recent/current service: With airlines worldwide including over 100 operators in the USA, 25 in the Middle East, Far East and Africa and four in Europe including Atlantic Airlines in the UK with a fleet of 11.
Recognition: The engines are positioned forward of the wing, close in to the fuselage. A low-set wing with swept leading edges and dihedral outboard of the engines, straight trailing edge and almost pointed wingtips. The oval fuselage is set above the wing with a distinctive rounded nose. The broad fin and rudder has a curved top. Mounted on either side of the fuselage below the fin, the tailplane has a swept front edge and straight trailing edge. The main undercarriage retracts into the lower part of the engine cowlings leaving one-third of the wheel exposed; the tailwheel does not retract.
Variants: Various modifications have been made to the DC-3 for VIP use with modified windows, powerplant refinements, nose radar and fully enclosed housings for the main wheels; cargo versions feature large 'double' doors on the port side of the rear fuselage. A Jet Prop DC-3AMI conversion is being undertaken in South Africa, powered by 1,424shp (1,062kW) PT6A-65ARs.

Below:
A DC-3 in the colours of Air Atlantique, which operates a fleet of 11. *PRM*

Embraer EMB-110 Bandeirante

Left:
The Bandeirante has a very angular appearance. *PRM*

Below:
The Brazilian EMB-110P1 Bandeirante is operated by commuter airlines on low density short-range routes.
Brian Strickland

Twin-turboprop commuter airliner

Basic data for EMB-110P2 Bandeirante

Powerplant: Two Pratt & Whitney PT6A-34 turboprops of 750shp (559kW)
Span: 50ft 3in (15.32m)
Length: 49ft 6in (15.01m)
Max Cruise: 244mph (393km/h)
Passengers: 18 plus two crew
First aircraft flown: 26 October 1968 (military version); 16 April 1973 (EMB-110C) and 3 May 1977 (EMB-110P2).
Production: 500 delivered worldwide to operators in 35 countries. Production ceased in September 1990.
Recent/current service: Used by 88 small operators worldwide, flying 214 examples as at the end of 1998.

Recognition: Twin turboprops project well forward of the low-set, straight wings with square wingtips. Straight fuselage sides with large rectangular cabin windows. The passenger doors are behind the cockpit and to the rear of the wing. A slightly swept angular fin and rudder has a dorsal extension; there is also a small ventral fin below the rear fuselage. The straight tailplane is set below the rudder on the fuselage cone.
Variants: The shorter EMB-110C is in limited use. The main variants are the stretched EMB-110P1 with a large rear cargo door and the EMB-110P2 with fore and aft passenger doors. EMB-110K1 is a lengthened all-cargo transport.

Left:
The streamlined Brasilia resembles the BAe Jetstream and Beech 1900. *PRM*

Below:
Many Brasilias are operated by US feeder/commuter airlines like United Express. *PRM*

Twin-turboprop regional airliner

Basic data for EMB-120ER

Powerplant: Two Pratt & Whitney Canada PW118A turboprops of 1,800shp (1,342kW)
Span: 64ft 10½in (19.78m)
Length: 65ft 7½in (20.0m)
Max Cruise: 313mph (504km/h)
Passengers: 30 with two crew
First aircraft flown: 27 July 1983.
Production: First delivery to US commuter airlines in July 1985 and DLT in Germany in January 1986. In late 1998 305 in airline service .
Recent/current service: Flown by 33 airlines including Air Exel Commuter, Atlantic SE AL, BASE Airlines, Comair, Continental Express, Danish Air Transport, Flandre Air, KLM exel, Luxair, Mesa AG, Regional AL, RioSul, Skywest, TAT European AL and West Air.

Recognition: Two turboprops projecting forward from the low-set, straight wings. The wings have a slight dihedral and the leading-edge is swept inboard of the engines. Slim, circular fuselage with a large swept fin and rudder with dorsal projection. The swept tailplane is located on top of the fin. Pointed nose with sharply raked large cockpit windscreens.
Variants: A 'hot-and-high' version with reduced structural weight and more powerful PW118A turboprops was launched in 1988. From August 1994, the standard production model was the EMB-120ERX, which has further interior improvements. EMB-120QC quick-change and EMB-120C cargo and combi versions are the other primary derivatives.

Fairchild Dornier 228

Twin-turboprop commuter airliner

Above:
This landing view shows the Dornier 228's unusual wing with its straight trailing-edge and curved leading-edge. *PRM*

Basic data for Fairchild Dornier 228-212

Powerplant: Two AlliedSignal Garrett TPE 331-5-252D turboprops of 776shp (579kW)

Span: 55ft 8in (16.97m)

Length: 54ft 4in (16.56m)

Max Cruise: 269mph (434km/h)

Passengers: 19 plus two crew

First aircraft flown: 28 March 1981 (Series 100) and 9 May 1981 (Series 200).

Production: 240 aircraft delivered when production ceased in 1995.

Recent/current service: 43 airlines worldwide fly 228s including Air Guadeloupe, Air Maldives, DANA, Highland Air, LGW, Martinair, Milne Bay Air, Olympic Aviation, Suckling AW and Vayudoot.

Recognition: Small turboprops mounted on the leading-edge of the 'new technology' wing which has a straight trailing-edge and curved leading-edge with pointed wingtips. The square, slab-sided fuselage is positioned below the wing. Forward of the cockpit the flat-bottomed nose is shaped downwards to give a 'drooped' appearance. The angular fin and rudder has a large dorsal fillet extending to the rear of the wing fairing. The flat tailplane is mounted below the rudder, extending beyond the fuselage cone. The main undercarriage retracts into lower fuselage fairings.

Variants: Series 100 has a fuselage of 49ft 3in (15.01m) for 15 passengers; the Series 200 has a 5ft (1.52m) longer fuselage for 19 passengers. The 203F freighter version has a 2,300kg payload. The 228-212 superseded all previous variants in 1990, with TPE 331-5A-25Ds; it has under-fuselage strakes.

Below:
The Fairchild Dornier 228 has a square-section fuselage and a crescent-shaped wing profile. *PRM*

Fairchild Dornier 328

Left:
Like the 228, the bigger 328 has a distinctive wing shape. *PRM*

Below:
The Fairchild Dornier 328 features a circular fuselage, a swept fin and rudder with a small 'T'-tail. *Peter Busby*

Twin-turboprop commuter airliner

Basic data for Fairchild Dornier 328-200

Powerplant: Two Pratt & Whitney Canada PW119B turboprops of 2,180shp (1,625kW)
Span: 68ft 10in (20.98m)
Length: 69ft 9½in (21.28m)
Max Cruise: 397mph (639km/h)
Passengers: 30-33 plus two crew
First aircraft flown: 6 December 1991.
Production: 71 delivered by late 1998 with a further 19 on order.
Recent/current service: The first 328 was delivered to the Swiss regional operator Air Engiadina in October 1993. Also in service with Euro City Line, Eurowings, Horizon AL, Lone Star AL, Minerva Italy, Proteus Air System, PSA Airlines, SATENA and Suckling AW.

Recognition: Small turboprops mounted on the leading-edge of the 'new technology' wing with pointed tips. Six-blade propellers. Circular fuselage is positioned below the high shoulder-wing. Swept fin and rudder with small T-tail and pointed rear fuselage cone. The main undercarriage retracts into lower fuselage fairing.
Variants: A stretched 48-passenger version with a laminar-flow wing is planned for the future. The Fairchild Dornier 328-110JET, powered by two P&W Canada PW306/9 turbofans, made its maiden flight on 20 January 1998.

Left:
Flown by US commuter airlines in particular, the Fairchild Metro III has a relatively long, thin, circular fuselage. *PRM*

Left:
The Fairchild Dornier Metro III has a noticeably long fuselage, especially to the rear of its wings. *PRM*

Twin-turboprop commuter airliner

Basic data for Metro III

Powerplant: Two Garrett TPE331-12UAR turboprops of 1,100shp (820kW)
Span: 57ft 0in (17.37m)
Length: 59ft 4¼in (18.09m)
Max Cruise: 317mph (511km/h)
Passengers: 19 plus two crew
First aircraft flown: 26 August 1969 (SA-226TC Metro); 31 December 1981 (Metro IIIA).
Production: Over 950 of all variants delivered by late 1998 including 20 Expediters.
Recent/current service: 408 Metros in scheduled service with 50 operators in 20 countries, mainly US commuter airlines.
Recognition: A long, slender circular section fuselage is mounted above the slightly tapered wings.

The twin turboprops extend well forward of the wings and are close into the fuselage. The raked fin and rudder appears small on the longer fuselage. The tailplane, set above the fuselage on the dorsal extension, is swept sharply.
Variants: Originally developed by Swearingen from the Beech Queen Air as the Merlin II, the pressurised Metro was built by Fairchild. The Metro II had larger windows and other refinements. The Metro III features a new wing of 10ft 9in (3.28m) greater span; the Expediter is an all-cargo version with a strengthened cabin floor. The Merlin IVC is a corporate version and the C-26A is a variant for the US Air National Guard. The 19-passenger Metro V, with TPE331-12s, is Fairchild's successor to the Metro III and includes a 'stand-up' cabin. The Metro 23 is an increased maximum take-off weight variant.

Left:
The high-wing Fairchild FH-227/Fokker F27 is powered by two R-R Dart turboprops.
PRM

Right:
A Fokker F27-600 Friendship of Jersey European.
PRM

Twin-turboprop regional airliner

Basic data for F27-500 Friendship

Powerplant: Two Rolls-Royce Dart 536-7R turboprops of 2,320shp (1,730kW)
Span: 95ft 2in (29.01m)
Length: 82ft 2½in (25.06m)
Max Cruise: 298mph (480km/h)
Passengers: 60 plus two crew
First aircraft flown: 24 November 1954 (Fokker F27); 12 April 1958 (Fairchild FH-227).
Production: Over 786 built when production ceased in 1985 including 206 in USA by Fairchild. Fokker production includes 85 Mk 100, 138 Mk 200, 13 Mk 300, 218 Mk 400/600, 112 Mk 500. Fairchild built 128 F27s and 78 FH-227s.
Recent/current service: 293 in service with 83 airlines in late 1998 including Air Algérie, Air France, BAC Express AL, Channel Express, Comair, Farner Air Transport, Jersey European, KLM uk, Libyan Arab, Merpati Nusantara, Mountain Air Cargo, Pakistan Int'l AL, TAAG Angola, TAM Bolivia and WDL Flugdienst.
Recognition: Twin turboprops set below the high, straight wing. A slender oval-section fuselage with a pointed nose and tail; the cabin windows are distinctively oval-shaped. A tall fin and rudder with a large dorsal extension. The small tailplane is set either side of the base of the rudder.
Variants: F27 Mk 200 (F27A) has improved powerplants; F27 Mk 300 (F27B) 'Combiplane' has a large forward cargo door; F27 Mk 400 (F27M) has improved powerplants; F27 Mk 500 has a 5ft (1.52m) longer fuselage and a large forward cargo door; F27 Mk 600 retains the shorter fuselage but has the other improvements of the Mk 500; FH227B to E has a 6ft (1.83m) longer fuselage of 83ft 8in (25.5m) and other improvements. Many have now been converted as freighters.

Fokker 50

Left/Below:
The Fokker 50 looks very similar to the earlier F27, but its new powerplant and six-blade propellers make it readily distinguishable. *PRM*

Twin-turboprop regional airliner

Basic data for Fokker 50-100

Powerplant: Two Pratt & Whitney Canada PW125B turboprops of 2,500shp (1,865kW)
Span: 95ft 1¾in (29.00m)
Length: 82ft 10in (25.25m)
Max Cruise: 332mph (535km/h)
Passengers: Maximum 46-58 plus two crew
First aircraft flown: 28 December 1985.
Production: Over 190 were delivered by the time of Fokker's bankruptcy in March 1996.
Recent/current service: 185 in service with 29 airlines in late 1998, including Aer Lingus Commuter, Air Iceland, Air Nostrum, Avianca, Contactair, Ethiopian AL, KLM Cityhopper, <u>KLM uk</u>, Luxair, Maersk, Malaysian AL, Norwegian Air Shuttle, Rio Sul, SAS Commuter, Skyways Sweden and Skywest.
Recognition: Little different from the F27-500 from which it is derived. Twin turboprops set below the high, straight wings. A slender, oval-section fuselage with a pointed nose and tail. A tall fin and rudder with a large dorsal extension. The small tailplane is set either side of the base of the rudder. Fokker 50 has smaller, rectangular cabin windows than F27-500.
Variants: The Series 300, introduced in 1993, is a 'hot-and-high' version. The Fokker 60UTA-N is a military utility version with 1.62m fuselage stretch; four are in use with the Royal Netherlands AF.

TWIN-ENGINED PROPELLER AIRLINERS

Ilyushin Il-114

Twin-turboprop short-range passenger and freight transport

Basic data for Il-114

Above:
The Russian Il-114 twin turboprop is similar in appearance to the BAe ATP/Jetstream 61. PRM

Powerplant: Two Isotov TV7-117C turboprops of 2,500shp (1,864kW) or Klimov Corporation TV7-117S
Span: 98ft 5½in (30.00m)
Length: 88ft 1in (26.86m)
Max Cruise: 310mph (500km/h)
Passengers: 64 plus two crew
First aircraft flown: 29 March 1990.
Production: Designed to meet an Aeroflot requirement, it is available to Western markets with Pratt & Whitney Canada PW127 turboprops. In production at the TAPO Tashkent plant in Uzbekistan. Production rate is intended to be 100 aircraft per year.

Recent/current service: Entered airline service in 1996.
Recognition: Slim circular fuselage (has no underfloor stowage). Twin turboprops mounted above and forward of the low-set wing, with undercarriage fairing beneath. Tall swept tailfin and rudder. Turboprops drive six-blade Stupino ultra-wide-chord low-noise CB-34 carbon-fibre composite propellers. Forward and rear entry doors on port side of fuselage. Twin wheels on each unit.
Variants: A cargo version has been developed with a rear cargo door and a 6-tonne payload. The Il-114PC is the version with PW127 turboprops, supplied by a Pratt & Whitney Canada/Klimov joint venture.

LET L-410 Turbolet

Left:
The Let L-410 has a short 'tubby' fuselage and high wings. *DJM*

Right:
The improved Let L-410UVP-E20 accommodates more passengers and has new engines driving five-blade propellers. *PRM*

Twin-turboprop regional airliner

Basic data for LET L-410UVP-E20

Powerplant: Two Motorlet M601E turboprops of 750shp (559kW)
Span: 65ft 6in (19.98m) over tip-tanks
Length: 47ft 4in (14.42m)
Max Cruise: 236mph (380km/h)
Passengers: 19 plus two crew
First aircraft flown: 16 April 1969; L-410UVP-E first flown 30 December 1984.
Production: Over 1,000 delivered as of late 1998.
Recent/current service: 645 are used by 77 carriers including Aeroflot Russian Int'l AL and its successor airlines, Skoda Air, Slov-Air and airlines in Brazil, Bulgaria, Denmark, Hungary, Libya and Poland.
Recognition: Engines mounted below and forward of the high-set, straight-leading-edge wing with wingtip tanks. A short, oval section fuselage with a long tapered nose forward of the cockpit. Seven rectangular cabin windows, with a large cabin door just aft of the wing. Large undercarriage fairings extend out from the lower fuselage. A slightly swept, tall, angular fin and rudder with a ventral extension below the tail cone. The straight, dihedralled tailplane is mounted on the fin above the fuselage.
Variants: Early production L-410A had Pratt & Whitney PT6A turbo-props; the L-410M introduced Motorlet M601 powerplants. The L-410UVP with a slightly larger fuselage, extended wingtips, taller fin and rudder and other detailed changes was produced until 1985. The L-410UVP-E20 accommodates four more passengers, has new engines driving five-blade propellers and wingtip fuel tanks. The UVP-E20 Model 420 first flew on 11 November 1993 and has more powerful M601E engines and other improvements. The L-430 is a proposed stretched version of the L-410 with Pratt & Whitney Canada PT6 turboprops.

LET L-610

Twin-turboprop short-haul regional transport

Basic data for LET L-610M

Above:
The larger Let L-610 has been designed for short-haul regional transport work and features a 'T'-tail. The longer, oval-section fuselage with 12 rectangular cabin windows and a large cabin door forward of the wing distinguishes the Let L-610 from the earlier L-410.

Powerplant: Two Motorlet M602 turboprops of 1,822shp (1,358kW) or two GE CT7-9Ds of 1,750shp (1,305kW)
Span: 84ft 0in (25.60m)
Length: 67ft 4¼in (20.53m)
Max Cruise: 289mph (466km/h)
Passengers: 40 plus two crew
First aircraft flown: 28 December 1988.
Production: Commenced 1990, but it is currently suspended.
Recent/current service: Not yet in regular commercial service.
Recognition: Engines mounted below and forward of the high-set wing. Oval-section fuselage with a long tapered nose forward of the cockpit. Twelve rectangular cabin windows with a large cabin door forward of the wing. Large undercarriage fairings extend out from the lower fuselage. A slightly swept, tall, angular fin and rudder. Tailplane without dihedral is mounted high on the fin.
Variants: A 48-passenger stretched version is under consideration. The 'westernised' L-610G, first flown on 18 December 1992, has General Electric CT7-9D 1,745shp (1,300kW) powerplants. The new owner of LET, Ayres Corporation is hoping to get European and US certification in early 1999.

Left:
The Raytheon Beech 1900D has its cabin height increased and larger windows compared with earlier versions. *PRM*

Below:
The Raytheon Beech 1900 is widely used by US commuter airlines. *PRM*

Twin-turboprop commuter airliner

Basic data for Beech 1900D

Powerplant: Two Pratt & Whitney Canada PT6A-67D turboprops of 1,279shp (953.75kW)
Span: 57ft 11½in (17.67m) over winglets
Length: 57ft 10in (17.65m)
Max Cruise: 320mph (515km/h)
Passengers: 19 plus two crew
First aircraft flown: 3 September 1982 (1900C); 1 March 1990 (1900D).
Production: Over 575 sold for airline and military use. Production of the 1900C stopped in 1991 when it was replaced by the 1900D.
Recent/current service: With many commuter airlines in the USA. In Europe with Air Express (Sweden), Air Littoral, Flandre Air and Proteus Air System.

Recognition: Twin turboprops mounted on a low wing. Slab-sided fuselage with small circular cabin windows. Stabilon horizontal surfaces mounted on fuselage, forward of the tailplane. A swept fin and rudder with both dorsal and vertical fillets. High-set swept tailplane with distinctive 'tail-lets' underneath.
Variants: The 1900D Airliner is the regional transport. Quick-change interior allows conversion from passenger to cargo configuration. 1900D Executive is the business version.

107

Reims Cessna F406 Caravan II

Twin-turboprop utility and feeder line aircraft

Above:
A number of Reims F406 Caravan IIs are in service with small airlines and air-taxi services. PRM

Basic Data for F406 Caravan II

Powerplant: Two Pratt & Whitney Canada PT6A-112 turboprops of 500shp (373kW)
Span: 49ft 5½in (15.08m)
Length: 39ft 0¼in (11.89m)
Max Cruise: 263mph (424km/h)
Passengers: 12 plus two crew
First aircraft flown: 22 September 1983.
Production: An executive development of the Cessna 404 Titan with two Pratt & Whitney turboprops built by Reims Aviation in France. Over 80 delivered and production continuing.
Recent/current service: With many smaller feeder airlines (41 customers in 28 countries).

Recognition: Developed from the Cessna Conquest airframe. Low-wing twin-engined monoplane. Single swept fin and rudder with dorsal fillet forward of fin. Square wingtips. Straight leading-edge to wing. Engine nacelles over wing protrude behind trailing-edge. Twin ventral strakes at rear. Dihedralled tailplane set midway up fin. Four oblong cabin windows, together with two smaller windows, on each side of fuselage.
Variants: Freight version (with underbelly cargo pod), target-towing and coastal patrol versions have been produced. Vigilant – a version for Scottish Fisheries Protection Agency with belly radome containing GEC Ferranti Seaspray 2000 radar.

Saab 340

Twin-turboprop regional airliner

Basic data for Saab 340B

Above:
The Saab 340 is widely used for commuter networks in the USA, such as the American Eagle operation for American Airlines. *PRM*

Powerplant: Two General Electric CT7-9B turboprops of 1,870shp (1,395kW)
Span: 70ft 4in (21.44m)
Length: 64ft 8¾in (19.73m)
Max Cruise: 325mph (522km/h)
Passengers: 30-37 plus two crew
First aircraft flown: 25 January 1983 (340); April 1989 (340B).
Production: The 340 line will close by mid-1999.
Recent/current service: 38 airlines fly 423 examples, these carriers including Air Nelson, AMR Eagle, British Midland Commuter, Business Express, Chautauqua AL, Crossair, Euro City Line, Express AL, Finnair, Formosa AL, Kendell, KLM City-Hopper, Japan Air Commuter, Lithuanian AL, Mesaba AL, Moldovan AL, Regional AL,

Shandong AL, Skyways and Tatra Air.
Recognition: Slim engines projecting forward of the low, straight wing which is set midway along the circular-section fuselage. A swept fin and rudder with a dorsal fillet projecting forward to the cabin windows. The small, dihedralled tailplane is mounted either side of the tail cone below the fin. The cockpit windscreen slopes down to the nose cone in a continuous line.
Variants: The 340B has an extended-span tailplane and more powerful engines. The 340'QC' (Quick Change) carries passengers during the day and containerised mail at night. Saab has introduced a faster 340B-based turboprop, using the Saab 2000 technology and called Saab 340B Plus with extended wingtips.

Saab 2000

Twin-turboprop regional airliner

Basic data for Saab 2000

Powerplant: Two Allison AE2100A turboprops of 4,152shp (3,095kW)
Span: 81ft 2¾in (24.76m)
Length: 89ft 6in (27.28m)
Max Cruise: 421mph (678km/h)
Passengers: 50 plus two crew
First aircraft flown: 26 March 1992.
Production: 51 delivered by late 1998, with a further 16 on order. Production will cease by mid-1999.
Recent/current service: Six airlines use 51 examples, among them Air Marshall Islands, Crossair, Regional AL and SAS Commuter.

Recognition: Similar to the Saab 340 but with a much longer fuselage. Slim engines projecting forward of the low, straight wing which has six flap runners on the underside. A circular-section fuselage with large fairings at the wing junction. A swept fin and rudder with a dorsal fillet projecting well forward. The tailplane is mounted at the base of fin. External ventral strakes run from the nose to the wing fairing. The cockpit windscreen slopes down to the nose cone in a continuous line.

Variants: A passenger/cargo combi version was introduced during the latter part of 1996.

Above/Left:
The Saab 2000 has a much longer fuselage than the Saab 340 and features large fairings at the wing junction. *PRM*

Left:
The Shorts 330 has a distinctive straight, narrow-chord wing, large rectangular fins and rudders and a 'box-like' fuselage. *PRM*

Below:
The very angular Shorts 330 is used for short domestic routes. *Paul Gingell*

Twin-turboprop regional airliner

Basic data for Shorts 330-200

Powerplant: Two Pratt & Whitney PT6A-45R turboprops of 1,198shp (893.3kW)
Span: 74ft 8in (22.76m)
Length: 58ft ½in (17.69m)
Max Cruise: 218mph (352km/h)
Passengers: 30 plus two crew
First aircraft flown: 22 August 1974 (SD3-30).
Production: 130 delivered (including 35 military versions). Production now ceased.

Recent/current service: 42 operate with Air Cargo Carriers, Air Caveral, Air Labrador, BAC Express AL, Corporate Air, Flying Enterprise, Ireland AW, Mountain Air Cargo and Streamline Aviation.

Recognition: Larger development of the Skyvan with the same general features including a slab-sided fuselage and twin fins and rudders. The top of the fuselage is noticeably humped and the nose and the rear sections are more streamlined. The undercarriage retracts, with the main wheels entering a fairing located either side of the fuselage below the wings.

Variants: Prototype SD3-30, renamed the 330-100 has 1,173shp PT6A-45B turboprops while the 330-200 has uprated 1,198shp PT6A-45Rs. The 330-UTT is a military utility development of the 330-200 used by the USAF as the C-23A Sherpa. The US Army National Guard version is the C-23B.

Shorts 360

Twin-turboprop regional airliner

Basic data for Shorts 360-300

Above/Below:
The larger Shorts 360 has a single fin and rudder, upgraded engines and six-blade propellers. PRM

Powerplant: Two Pratt & Whitney PT6A-67R turboprops of 1,424shp (1,062kW)
Span: 74ft 10in (22.81m)
Length: 70ft 10in (21.59m)
Max Cruise: 242mph (390km/h)
Passengers: 39 plus two crew
First aircraft flown: 1 June 1981.
Production: 164 delivered when production ceased June 1991.
Recent/current service: Some 118 with 37 airlines in late 1998, including Air Cargo Carriers, AMR Eagle, Aurigny, BAC Express AL, British Regional AL, Executive AL, RedEx, Flying Enterprise, Gill AW, Hazelton, Holmstroem Air Sweden, Jersey European, Muk Air, Pacific Island Aviation, Sunstate AL and Titan AW.

Recognition: A refined development of the Shorts 330 with a 3ft (0.91m) longer fuselage forward of the wing, and a distinctive, tall, single fin and rudder, set on top of the tapered upswept rear fuselage. The wing-shape, forward fuselage, bracing struts, retractable undercarriage and powerplants are similar to the Shorts 330.
Variants: Externally all versions are similar. The 360-300 has upgraded engines and six-blade propellers.

AÉROSPATIALE SE210 CARAVELLE

Twin-turbojet short-range airliner

Powerplant: Two Rolls-Royce Avon 532 turbojets of 12,600lb st (56kN)
Span: 112ft 6in (34.29m)
Length: 108ft 3½in (33.01m)
Max Cruise: 525mph (845km/h)
Passengers: 139 plus three crew
First aircraft flown: 25 May 1955 (Caravelle I).

Above: Only a handful of Caravelles remain in service with French operators. *Paul Ridgwell*

There were nearly a dozen variants of the Caravelle, 282 being built between 1955 and 1973. The initial I, IA and III are externally the same; the only visual difference of the VI-N is the noise suppressors fitted to the engines, while the VI-R had thrust reversers. The Caravelle 10B had a 3ft 4in (1.02m) longer fuselage, revised wing leading edge and modified flaps; the 11R had a front fuselage freight loading door; and the Super Caravelle 12 had a further 10ft (3.05m) fuselage stretch and was re-engined with Pratt & Whitney JT8D turbofans. Seventeen remain in service as of late 1998.

AUDREY PROMOTIONS/ B-N TRI-COMMUTER/ TRISLANDER

Three-piston-engine short-range commuter transport

Powerplant: Three Textron Lycoming 0-540-E4C piston engines of 260hp (193.9kW)
Span: 53ft 0in (16.14m)
Length: 49ft 3in (15.01m)
Max Cruise: 166mph (267km/h)
Passengers: 18 plus one crew
First aircraft flown: 11 September 1970.

Above: The 17-seat Trislander is the only tri-piston-engine airliner flying scheduled services. *PRM*

A total of 73 were built by 1982, prior to production switching to Audrey Promotions in Australia. Currently in service with Aurigny Air Service, XP Express and some small US commuter airlines.

AIRLINERS IN BRIEF

GRUMMAN GULFSTREAM I

Twin-turboprop commuter airliner

Above: The Gulfstream I is mainly used as a corporate aircraft but is also operated as a commuter airliner. *APM*

Powerplant: Two Rolls-Royce Dart 529-8X turboprops of 2,210shp (1,648kW)
Span: 78ft 4in (23.88m)
Length: 63ft 9in (19.43m)
Max Cruise: 340mph (560km/h)
Passengers: 37 plus two crew
First aircraft flown: 14 August 1958.

Over 200 Gulfstream Is were built between 1958 and 1963, and nearly one-third are in airline service today. AMR Eagle operates a stretched version. Mainly used as a corporate aircraft but also being operated as a commuter airliner.

NAMC YS-11

Twin-turboprop regional airliner

Above: The Japanese NAMC YS-11 remains in service with a handful of commuter airlines. *PRM*

Powerplant: Two Rolls-Royce Dart 527 turboprops of 3,060shp (2281.8kW)
Span: 105ft 0in (32.00m)
Length: 86ft 3½in (26.30m)
Max Cruise: 256mph (412.9km/h)
Passengers: 52-60 plus two crew
First aircraft flown: 23 October 1964.

Sixty-six of the 182 YS-11s built by the Japanese consortium remain in airline service in late 1998.

PIPER NAVAJO/ CHIEFTAIN

Twin-piston/ turboprop light transport

Powerplant: Two Lycoming T10-540 piston engines of 350shp (261kW)
Span: 40ft 8in (12.40m)
Length: 36ft 8in (11.18m)
Max Cruise: 254mph (409km/h)
First aircraft flown: 30 September 1964.

Above: More powerful than early Piper twins, the Navajo is used for short commuter and air taxi services. *PRM*

Some 2,500 examples of the Navajo series were built and are in service with air taxi and commuter airlines worldwide and particularly in the USA. The Chieftain is 2ft (0.61m) longer, with a modified nose and cabin.

PZL-MIELEC (ANTONOV) AN-2

Single-piston-engined general-purpose biplane

Powerplant: One PZL Kalisz ASz-621R piston engine of 1,000hp (746kW) or one Shevetsov ASR-621R
Span: Upper: 59ft 7¼in (18.18m) Lower: 46ft 8½in (14.42m)
Length: 41ft 9½in (12.74m)
Max Cruise: 115mph (185km/h)
First aircraft flown: 31 August 1947.

Above: The PZL-Mielec (Antonov) An-2 is still widely used around the world. *PRM*

Over 5,000 examples were built in the Soviet Union. Limited production continues in China and Poland (with over 12,000 built). Currently many An-2Rs, the 12-seat passenger version, are used in Third World countries as a transport. Uzbekistan Airways' Tashkent repair base has developed a restoration programme for the An-2.

AIRLINERS IN BRIEF

SHORT BELFAST

Four-turboprop medium/long-range cargo transport

Powerplant: Four Rolls-Royce Tyne RTy12 turbo-props of 5,730shp (4,273kW)
Span: 158ft 10in (48.82m)
Length: 136ft 5in (41.69m)
Max Cruise: 352mph (566km/h)
First aircraft flown: 5 January 1964.

Above: A pair of ex-RAF Belfasts are flown by HeavyLift for transporting outsize freight loads. *PRM*

Ten were built for the RAF and three were converted for civil use. Currently in service with HeavyLift Cargo AL.

YAKOVLEV YAK-40

Three-turbofan short/medium-range regional airliner

Powerplant: Three Ivchenko AI-25 turbofans of 3,300lb st (14.7kN)
Span: 82ft 0¼in (25.0m)
Length: 66ft 9in (20.36m)
Max Cruise: 342mph (550km/h)
Passengers: 24-32 plus two crew
First aircraft flown: 21 October 1966.

Above: The small three-engined Yak-40 is mainly used as a feeder airliner in the Russian Federation area. *PRM*

Total production of 1,011 when the final version was delivered in 1985. Some 570 remain in service, mainly as a feeder airliner in the Russian Federation area and also as VIP transports in several countries, but nearly half of this total are reputed to be in storage at airfields across Russia and the former Soviet republics.

Seen from the same angle many airliners can appear very much alike and it becomes quite difficult to tell one type from another. Here is a selection of photographs of airliners which are superficially similar, together with a key to their individual recognition features to help you distinguish them.

Above: Airbus A300-600R. *PRM*

Above: Airbus A310-304. *PRM*

Airbus A300/A310
Key recognition feature: The shorter fuselage of the A310 which gives it a more 'dumpy' appearance. The A300's fuselage is noticeably longer forward of the wing.
Other features: The A310 has three underwing fences/flap fairings outboard of each engine while the A300 has four.

SIMILAR SHAPES

Above: Douglas DC-10. *PRM*

Above: McDonnell Douglas MD-11. *PRM*

Above: Lockheed TriStar. *DJM*

McDonnell Douglas DC-10/MD-11 and Lockheed TriStar

Key recognition feature: The third, fin-mounted rear engine. The DC-10's engine is positioned clear of the rear fuselage and has a straight-through jet pipe with a small extension of the fin on the top surface. The MD-11 can be recognised by its winglets and has a longer fuselage than the DC-10. The TriStar's third engine intake is moulded on to the top of the fuselage and the front of the fin. It exhausts through the fuselage tail cone aft of the tailplane.
Other features: The TriStar has a more shaped nose than the DC-10 and a broader-chord fin.

Above: Boeing 757. PRM

Above: Boeing 767. PRM

Boeing 757/767
Key recognition feature: The longer-looking 'pencil' fuselage of the 757 compared with the 'fatter' fuselage of the 767. The 757 has a much longer fuselage section forward of the wing than the 767.
Other features: The nose of the 757 has a flatter underside which gives it a more 'dropped' appearance than the 767's more rounded look.

Above: ATR42-300. *DJM*

Above: Dash 8-300. *PRM*

Avions de Transport Regional ATR 42/Bombardier (De Havilland) Dash 8

Key recognition feature: The ATR 42 has a straight line to its lower fuse-lage, raising to a conical tail cone, whereas the Dash 8 has a more streamlined swept-up rear fuselage with no tail cone, but with a more pronounced dorsal fillet ahead of the fin. The engine nacelles of the Dash 8 protrude well behind the trailing-edge of the wing, while the ATR 42's are more flush.

Other features: The ATR 42 has lower-fuselage 'bumps' to house the main undercarriage, whereas the Dash 8's main wheels retract into the engine nacelles. Flap brackets are very noticeable along the trailing-edges of the ATR 42's wings and its tailplane is set just below the top of the fin, while the Dash 8's sits on the top.

Above: Airbus A300-600R. *PRM*

Above: Boeing 767-300ER. *PRM*

Airbus A300/Boeing 767
Key recognition feature: The number of spoilers extending below the wing. The Airbus A300 has five very pronounced underwing fences/flap fairings while the Boeing 767 has only three.

Other features: The Airbus has a more circular-section fuselage than the 767 and a straight top to the rear fuselage. The 767's fin is taller and narrower-chord than the A300's and it has a more triangular-shaped tailplane.

Above: Fokker 100. *DJM*

Above: Douglas DC-9-32. *PRM*

Fokker 100/McDonnell Douglas DC-9

Key recognition feature: The DC-9's wing has more pronounced leading-edge slats than the Fokker 100's while the latter has three pronounced fences/flap fairings on each trailing-edge.

Other features: The Fokker 100 has a rectangular end to the fuselage which opens as air brakes. The DC-9 does not have this feature, its tail cone being pointed. The Fokker 100 also has a pronounced dorsal extension to its shorter and broader fin, which has a curved top.

Above: Boeing 707-369C. *PRM*

Above: Douglas DC-8-73F. *APM*

Boeing 707/McDonnell Douglas DC-8
Key recognition feature: The DC-8 has a slimmer looking fuselage with a longer nose forward of the cockpit.
Other features: The Boeing 707 has a Pitot tube projecting forward from the top of its fin; the DC-8's fin is more swept and tapered than the 707's. The DC-8 has fewer, but larger, windows that are more widely spaced than the 707's. The DC-8 has landing lights in the nose.

Above: Boeing 737-300. *DJM*

Above: Airbus A320.

Boeing 737-300/Airbus A320

Key recognition feature: The slimmer looking 'oval' fuselage of the A320-200 compares with the 'fatter', circular fuselage of the B737-300. While the B737's wings are midway along the fuselage, the A320's wing is further forward, giving the impression of a shorter fuselage.

Other features: The A320 has a pronounced fillet at the rear of its wing where it joins the fuselage. The B737 has its landing lights in the wing inboard of the engines. The A320's lights are at the top of the nosewheel undercarriage leg.

Above: Airbus A330. *PRM*

Above: Boeing 777. *PRM*

Airbus A330/Boeing 777

Key recognition feature: The A330 has four wing trailing-edge fairings whereas the Boeing 777 has three. The upper fuselage line continues level under the fin of the A330 but tapers downwards on the Boeing 777. Winglets are fitted to the A330 but not to the Boeing 777. Though the fuselage lengths are nearly identical the A330 appears longer and slimmer.

Other features: The A330 has twin main-wheel bogies whereas the Boeing 777 features unique triple bogies.

INDEX